Women, Law and Public Opinion

Women, Law and Public Opinion

KRISHNA GUPTA

RAWAT PUBLICATIONS
Jaipur and New Delhi

ISBN 81-7033-642-2

Published by
Prem Rawat for ***Rawat Publications***
Satyam Apartments, Sector 3, Jain Temple Road,
Jawahar Nagar, Jaipur 302 004 India
Phone: 0141 651748 / 657006 Fax: 0141 651748
email: rawatbooks@pinkline.net

Delhi Office
G-4, 4832/24, Ansari Road, Darya Ganj, New Delhi 110 002
Phone: 3263290

Typeset by Rawat Computers, Jaipur
Printed at Nice Printing Press, New Delhi

Contents

Contents

Foreword

Dr. Krishna Gupta's book offers a theoretical and empirical examination of the relationship between law and public opinion in the realm of women's rights. She has focussed on two critical issues affecting the lives of women in very different contexts—the abortion debate in the United States, and the Hindu Code Bill and Dowry Prohibition Act in India. She concludes that public opinion has been ahead of enacted law and judicial opinion in the United States. Critical US judicial decisions upholding the right of abortion, followed a swing in opinion in favour of the right to choose. Judicial and legislative limitations on the right to choose abortion followed when the pendulum of opinion swung back. Judicial limitations on abortion rights gave expression to public doubts that full abortion rights, covering all stages of the foetal cycle, flow from the right to choose, and that all motives for abortion are legitimate. In the US, the nexus between law and opinion was tight.

Dr. Gupta's book also deals with the relationship between

law and opinion in India. When, in the 1950s and 1960s, Jawahar Lal Nehru and other Indian law-makers tried to use the law in the form of the Hindu Code Bill as an instrument of public education and social transformation, they failed, because law was too far ahead of public opinion. Nehru and his collaborators succeeded only when they tailored the law to take into account then current patriarchally skewed opinion. The deep gap between the original Hindu Code Bill and adverse public opinion required modification and dilution of the original bill. Dr. Gupta also shows how and why the Dowry Prohibition Act has been virtually a dead letter because its provisions were ahead of public opinion.

This well-researched book allows scholars of feminism to consider the Indian and American policies in a comparative framework. It also casts an interesting new light on an enduring question for political and legal thinkers from Aristotle to Dicey to Benegal Rao: What should be the relationship between law, public opinion and social reform? What Indian and American settings have in common is that democratic public opinion continues to be conservative. It has been difficult in both the settings to mobilise public opinion to change the patriarchal structure of legal and administrative arrangements. In both countries women's capacity to take command of their bodies and mind remains restricted.

Susanne Hoeber Rudolph
Department of Political Science
University of Chicago

Acknowledgements

I am deeply indebted to my friends and well-wishers who have helped me in the creation of this book. The idea of working on the correlation between law and public opinion was first mooted by Prof. Lloyd Rudolph. Being keenly interested in gender studies, I decided to examine their complex interaction in relation to the status of women in a comparative framework. Prof. Susanne Rudolph, Director, South Asia Centre, University of Chicago, has not only guided me but helped me at every step in the completion of this project. My deep gratitude to her for the immense support and her willingness to contribute a Foreword to this book. I am also grateful to Prof. Pradeep Mehendiratta, Director General and Vice President, American Institute of Indian Studies, New Delhi, for helping me to go to the University of Chicago as a visiting scholar. Prof. Ralph W. Nicholas, Professor of Anthropology and Director, International House of Chicago, most generously hosted my stay at the International House. The intermingling of ethnic cultures and communities and the warm hospitality I received at this hostel was an enriching experience. Mr. Jim Nye and his associates at the Regenstein Library were very helpful. Prof. Mary Becker of Chicago Law School encouraged and helped me in my research work. I owe my special thanks to my friends Indra and Roshan Goel and Diwakar Sundi for their great moral support during my stay. My earnest thanks to all my friends at the International House, Chicago for helping in several ways through this venture.

I am also thankful to CWDS Library, New Delhi, the American Central Libraries, Calcutta and New Delhi, and the Indian Institute of Advanced Study, Shimla for help and assistance. The initial script was meticulously typed by Mr. G.S. Sharma on the computer. Mr. Pranit Rawat very kindly agreed to publish this book.

Finally, I proudly remember my brother-in-law Late Rajendra Gupta of S. Chand & Company, New Delhi for inspiring and motivating me to undertake this task. I dedicate this book to his memory.

Krishna Gupta

Abbreviations

AIR	All India Reporter
Cri LJ	Criminal Law Journal (India)
SC	Supreme Court
SCC	Supreme Court Cases India
BBCJ	Journal of Bihar Bar Council
Cr.PC	Criminal Procedure Code
DVCM	Dahej Virodhi Chetna Manch
DPA	Dowry Prohibition Act
EPW	Economic and Political Weekly
IPC	Indian Penal Code
LSD	Lok Sabha Debates
HCB	Hindu Code Bill
MP	Member of Parliament
ERA	Equal Right Act
MTP	Medical Termination of Pregnancy
PFA	Platform for Action

I

Law and Public Opinion

The relationship between law and public opinion, though complex, is of great significance in liberal democracy. For, democracy is defined as a government which responds to the demands of the people. In fact, the legitimacy of the democratic regime depends on the support of the people. Hence, public opinion constitutes a key variable in a democratic polity. V.O. Key had asserted, "unless mass views have some place in the shaping of policy, all the talk about democracy is nonsense."[1] Political responses of the people are registered as public opinion, and these preferences of the people influence state policies. Social scientists have pondered over the problem whether law leads or lags behind public opinion. Ideally in a democratic system law follows public opinion. But sometimes law becomes an instrument of social change and tries to lead public opinion. The controversy between those who believe that law should essentially follow, not lead, and that it

1. Key, V.O., 1961, *Public Opinion and American Democracy*, New York: Alfred A. Knopf.

should do so slowly, in response to clearly formulated social sentiment, and those who believe that the law should be a determining agent in the creation of new norms, is one of the recurrent themes of the history of legal thought.[2]

Law, according to Aristotle, was a dispassionate reason and represented social experience, wisdom and social conscience. He stressed the educative value of law. Law, to him, was a rule of life, such as will make the members of a polis good and just.[3]

Analytical jurisprudence regards law as a formal means of social control by a political community. It believes that law emanates from a single authority in the state. However, law cannot exert social control unless it embodies the values which the people cherish. Thus, law must embody both value and validity.[4] The sociological approach regards law as located in society, reflecting social norms, serving social purpose. It emphasises the social character of law and maintains that it can become a vehicle of social change. To become an effective instrument of change, law must be based on social sense of rightness, and social justice must be in tune with public sentiments.

Legal instruments are social institutions and thus are part of the social organisation and culture. Law reflects social beliefs and preferences, gives expression to the values and specifies appropriate conduct.[5]

---

2. Friedmann, W., 1972, *Law in a Changing Society*, London: Stevens and Sons.
3. Barker, E., (ed. and trans.), 1968, *The Politics of Aristotle*, London: Oxford University Press.
4. Barker, E., 1967, *Principles of Social and Political Theory*, London: Oxford University Press.
5. Davis, K., 1949, *Human Society*, New York: Macmillan.

The instrumentalist approach, associated with Jeremy Bentham and Rudolf Von Jhering, among the nineteenth century writers, as well as Roscoe Pound of the USA, calls for the assessment of law according to defined social goals and purposes. Fuller understanding of law requires that it is studied in the social context in which it functions.

Bentham firmly believed in the efficacy of rationally construed reforming laws. It was his philosophy which turned the British parliament and similar institutions in other countries, into active legislative instruments, initiating social reforms in response to social needs. Law, according to Pound, is the body of knowledge and experience, with the aid of which social engineering is carried on. It is a science which is always seeking new instruments, new expedients, for new needs, new goods and for the good life.[6] He agreed with Justice Cardozo that, the function of law, is to promote the welfare of society.[7] There are two elements in this theory: one is the law making process, and the other is the administration of law. Greater emphasis must be placed on proper enforcement of law, so that it can truly become a means of social, economic and cultural progress of humanity.

On the other hand, Savingny was a bitter critic of the trends towards codification of law and held that law was 'found' and not made. His theory is today a matter of history, out of tune with the modern society. A century later, the Austrian jurist Eugene Ehrlich propagated the concept of the

---

6. Pound, Roscoe, 1959, *Jurisprudence*, Vol. I, Minnesota: West Publishing Co.; St. Paul, 1942, *Social Control Through Law*, New Haven: Yale University Press; 1923, *Interpretations of Legal History*, New York: Macmillan.
7. Cardozo, B.N., 1921, *The Nature of the Judicial Process*, New Haven: Yale University Press.

living law of people based on social behaviour rather than the compulsive norms of the state.[8] Law is often, perhaps usually dependent on other social institutions for its effective implementation. Legal rules must have the support of public sentiment. If laws are contrary to the sense of rightness of a people, they become difficult to enforce.[9] To retain public support, laws must be reasonable, in consonance with the current beliefs, and practices and must be accepted as part of the culture.[10] When public sentiment is not in agreement with the legal rules, the enforcement patterns give only nominal support to the written laws.[11] When legally mandated social change runs counter to internalised expectations, some people seek ways to circumvent the law. Summer viewed law as a wholly passive instrument that could never move ahead of the customs and mores of the people, and he believed that legislation that is not firmly rooted in popular folkways may force people to comply but cannot win their hearts.[12] Following Sumner, sociologists have often emphasised that the folkways and mores can thus nullify law, and jurists have

---

8. Friedmann, W., supra note 2.
9. Cave, F.A., "State, Law and Government", in Roucek, J.S., (ed.), 1947, *Social Control*, New York: D. Van Nostrand Co. Inc.; Ross, E.A., 1901, *Social Control: A Survey of the Foundations of Order*, New York: Macmillan.
10. Hiller, E.T., 1941, *Social Relations and Social Structures*, New York: Harper; MacIver, R.M., 1947, *Society*, New York: Holt, Rinehart and Winston; Cuber, J.F., 1951, *Sociology*, New York: Apleton Century Crofts.
11. Davis, F.J., "Law in Operation", in Davis, F.J., Foster, H.H., Jr., Jeffery, C.R., and Davis, E.E., (eds.), 1962, *Society and the Law*, USA: The Free Press of Glencoe.
12. Sumner, W.G., "On the Mores" in Parsons, T., (ed.), 1969, *Theories of Society*, New York: The Press.

called this, "the derogatory force of custom".[13] According to Emile Durkheim, as societies grew larger and more heterogeneous, social consensus could no longer be taken for granted.[14] The function of law changed from being a reflection of generally accepted customs to being a means of preserving harmonious relationship and reconciling diverse customs and interests.

Julius Stone[15] has identified three situations in which law may lack the support of public opinion. First, when the dominant public sentiment about a given situation may change while the laws remain unchanged, thus representing a cultural lag. Sometimes, laws lead cultural lags, when public sentiment remains unchanged while the law changes. In the third situation, the issues are so complex and ill understood, that the relation of laws to life situations is obscured and people are frustrated because they cannot understand what the government is doing and why. Laws, lacking public support, remain ineffective. But outdated values and traditions and irrational customs must be changed. In such situations law must play a dominant role in modifying obsolete customary ideas and bringing about uniform social change. The object of law is to help the progress of the community and meet the socio-economic challenges which vary from time to time. It has to educate people into accepting new values. Much of empirical research has challenged the Summerian concept of the inviolability of mores, and establishes that, "law can and does

---

13. Davis, F.J., supra note 11.
14. Durkheim, E., 1960, *The Division of Labour in Society*, Glencoe, III: Free Press; Parsons, Talcott, 1965, *Unity and Diversity in the Modern Intellectual Disciplines: The Role of the Social Sciences*, Daedalus.
15. Stone, Julius, 1950, *The Province and Function of Law*, Cambridge: Harvard University Press.

manipulate our deep-rooted attitudes and personalities."[16]

Growing Importance of Social Legislations in Liberal Democracies

Social legislations have already become the preponderant part of law in the modern state. They seek to bridge the gulf between the existing laws and the current need of society. They reflect the values and aspirations of a society, try to correct social imbalances, provide a protective umbrella to the weaker and deprived sections, and give a positive direction to social order. Legislation has assumed great importance as a democratic means of making new law to keep up with changing conditions and values. It can be used as an instrument for striking out in new directions and can, therefore, be a cultural lead as well as a cultural drag. It is difficult to enforce new laws if they are opposed to entrenched mores. Hence laws must be accompanied by change in social mores and attitudes. Hence, social legislation must be preceded and followed by social awakening and social consciousness.[17]

Public Opinion and Democracy

Public opinion is an essential prerequisite of social legislation. In a democracy, the interplay between law and public opinion is very close and complex. The key element of a democratic government is that it must take into account the wishes of the people. Following the Protestant Reformation and the Renaissance in Europe, popular opinion was increasingly seen as

---

16. Muir, W.K. Jr., 1967, *Law and Attitude Change*, Chicago: Chicago University Press.
17. Foster, Jr., Henry, H., "Public Law and Social Change", in Davis, J.F., Foster, H.H., Jr., Jeffery, C.R. and Davis, E.E., (eds.), 1962, *Society and the Law*, USA: The Free Press of Glencoe.

playing a part in governmental decisions. Machiavelli believed that princes should take this opinion into account in their calculations. By the 17th and the 18th century, leading political philosophers began recognising its significance. Rousseau held that all laws were ultimately based on public opinion and regarded the free expression of it as a major safeguard against despotism. Bentham stressed that the legislator could not ignore it. By the 19th century, the concept of public opinion had entered into the mainstream of political theory. In Europe, it was frequently seen as a weapon of the middle class against the old order.

Public opinion claims to be the voice of the people, that Locke sought to safeguard. It emerged at a specific historical moment, and became the most powerful symbol in the social and historical convulsions which shook Europe in the 18th and throughout the 19th century.[18] There are two viewpoints, one regards public opinion as the product of a permanent state of mind or collective consciousness. In this perspective public is taken to be the totality of individuals in society, viewed as a stable entity. Contrary to this, the second viewpoint regards such a conception as extremely hypothetical, for public opinion is a diverse and ever changing form of social expression.[19]

The situational perspective regards public as the collection of individuals who actually form and express opinions on a specific issue at a particular time. This perspective ex-

---

18. Peters, John, Durham, "Historical Tensions in the Concept of Public Opinion and the Communication of Consent", in Glasser, T.L. and Salmon, C.T., (eds.), 1995, *Public Opinion and the Communication of Consent*, New York: The Guilford Press.
19. Bennett, W.L., 1980, *Public Opinion in American Politics*, USA: Harcourt Brace, Javanovich, Inc.

plains variations in public opinion as the result of interactions between the beliefs and values of individuals and social and political conditions. Public opinion results when individuals seek expression through mass communication channels in order to participate meaningfully in political and cultural affairs.[20] Opinions are not just abstract political forces, they are the ultimate expressions for social acceptance, group pressures, membership identification and psychological needs. The study of public opinion is concerned with how people form and share judgements about problems, goals and issues. Public opinion has its roots in individual belief systems, social relations, communication technologies, cultural tradition and political processes.

Most of the definitions focus on two characteristics:

(1) Public opinion as rationality—it is instrumental in the process of opinion formation and decision making in a democracy.

(2) Public opinion as social control—its role in promoting social integration by basing actions and decisions on a sufficient level of social consensus.[21]

Some studies (Lippmann, 1922, 1925; Lasswell, 1927) show that public opinion is ignorant and uninformed. Earlier, Alexis-de-Tocqueville (1835, 1840, 1969) saw in public opinion a potential tyrant while J.S. Mill (1859, 1952) saw public opinion as a suffocating force of conformity, "a collective mediocrity". This liberal ambivalence towards public opinion continues to be part of our thinking about the public, in the

---

20. Bennett, W.L., Ibid.
21. Neumann, E.N., "Public Opinion and Rationality", in Glasser, T.C. and Salmon, C.T., (eds.), 1995, *Public Opinion and the Communication of Consent*, New York: The Guilford Press.

opinion of Habermas. Some empirical studies indicate that public is capable of making informed judgements and rational choices (Page and Shapiro, 1992; Tom Smith, 1994). Other researchers indicate that public opinion is unstable and changing, while other findings support the argument that opinion may be remarkably stable.

A democratic government is formed on the consent of the governed. The basis of the American government, according to Jefferson, is the opinion of the people. Public opinion, though sometimes momentarily led astray, was self correcting and the only legitimate censor of government.[22] This Jeffersonan view of public opinion is reflected in various theories of democracy (Sartori, 1987) and in various working models of American politics (Bennett, 1980; Corbett, 1991). Observers of the United States held that public opinion there rested on a far wider population base. James Bryce, writing in the 1880 described the American system as government by public opinion and believed that popular attitudes were expressed primarily by the press, political parties and elections.

The model of democracy implies that public opinion will be translated by decision makers into public policy representing the public good. Translation of public opinion into public policy is aided by certain linking mechanisms. In classical democratic theory, elections were considered as the primary linking mechanism. Additionally, a linking role has also been formulated for political parties, interest groups and mass media. Public opinion can influence public policy if three conditions are satisfied. First, the opinion expressed about important matters of public policy must be well in-

22. Lipscomb, A. (ed.), 1905, *The Writing of Thomas Jefferson*, Vol. 20, Washington D.C., Thomas Jefferson Memorial Association of the United States (original work written in 1787).

formed. Second, the distribution of public opinion must remain fairly stable over time. Third, it is often argued that strong and constant principles must underlie public thinking about different issues.

In the USA, following the presidential elections in 1936, measurement of opinions based on polling representative samples of larger populations came into prominence. By 1965, public opinion polling had spread throughout the world. These opinion polls have enabled social scientists to study how opinions vary between social groups, between countries, and over time. Such polls bring into public realm the voices of people who would otherwise go unheard, establish direct contact with the respondents, and enable policy makers to keep in touch with the public mood. Such poll analyses and studies seek to understand the interplay between public opinion and public policy, and social legislation.

Democracy nowadays is greatly influenced by political elites—those who have direct access to political power, organisational resources, knowledge and expertise, as well as communication channels. Citizens are generally more interested in private than in public issues. Hence, elites manipulate and influence public opinion through mass communication and propaganda. Elites include politicians, spokespersons of interest groups, high-level government officials, journalists, activists, experts and policy specialists. Issues are often sponsored, defined and promoted by these elites for advancing their agendas and group interests (Gamson, 1988).

Public opinion must, therefore, be viewed as representing complex social and political processes that involve individuals, groups, organisations as well institutions, and establish and maintain their dominance over the masses.

Interaction between Law and Public Opinion

There is a complex interaction between law and public opinion. According to the functionalists, law is a means of preserving harmonious social relationships and reconciling diverse customs and interests. Law was a response to the ambivalence created by the society's increasing complexity. The conflict theorists on the other hand, view law as a manipulative device of the powerful elites to establish and maintain their dominance over the classes in a society. The emphasis is on power relationships, which are made legitimate by law.[23]

Relation between law and public opinion is complex but of great significance in understanding the functioning of democratic systems. It if often difficult to say whether opinion has done most to produce a legislation or laws have created a climate conducive to the formation of opinion in support of such legislation. Dicey's study[24] explores the close interdependence between law and public opinion. In advanced civilisations, opinion dictates legislative change. Dicey endorsed Hume's view that the opinion of the governed is the real foundation of all government. Public opinion is generally constituted by habits and customary rules. Sometimes convictions of a small number of influential individuals may mould laws and institutions.

Another important fact highlighted by Dicey is that society legislates not on the basis of opinion but in accordance with their interest. Public opinion is far less the result of reasoning or of argument than of the circumstances in which

23. Hozoa, Winnie, 1990, *The Social and Legal Status of Women: A Global Perspective*, New York: Praeger.
24. Dicey, A.V., 1905, *Law and Public Opinion in England during the Nineteenth Century*, UK: Macmillan, First Indian Reprint, 1996, New Delhi: Universal.

men are placed. The condemnation of slavery in the northern states of the American Republic, and the apologies for slavery in the south, must be referred to difference of circumstances. But interest is itself governed by opinion. Hence in the ultimate analysis, opinion controls legislation.

In England, during the last 75 years, public opinion had exercised a direct control over legislation. However, in United States, constitution limits the power of both the Congress and the state legislatures and therefore prevents quick alteration of legislation in response to public opinion.

There exists at any given time, a body of beliefs, convictions, sentiments, accepted principles or firmly rooted prejudices which taken together, make up the public opinion. The large currents of public opinion which determine legislation, acquire force and volume only by degrees, and are in their turn liable to be checked or superceded by other counter currents or cross currents of opinion. Sometimes, the opinion which affects the development of the law has in modern England atleast, often originated with some single thinker or school of thinkers.

Opinion is influenced by the circumstances in which people are placed. The development of public opinion generally, and therefore of legislative opinion, has been in England at once gradual, or slow, and continuous.

Sometimes laws foster or create law making opinion. They affect the sentiments and convictions of the people. The belief that women must be given substantial legal equality has encouraged legislations to produce such equality. Social legislations in turn have influenced the social opinion of the country. However, Dicey holds that law and opinion are so intermixed that it is difficult to say whether the opinion produced legislations or laws create a legislative opinion.[25]

Often people are influenced by habits rather than by thought. In a democratic system, law must generally respond to the irresistible tide of social habit and opinion.[26] When legally mandated social change runs counter to internalised expectations, people resist the new laws. Formal grant of equal rights were not able to secure women's substantive participation. For example, in the 1940s and 1950s, a large number of American women joined the labour force, won legal rights, yet the traditional belief that women were primarily homemakers remained largely unchanged. Structural barriers to gender equality remained and women remained clustered in all the lowest paying jobs. But, as a new patterns of gender, role activity became an accomplished fact in the western societies, it eventually affected some attitudes and behaviour.

Often the opinion which leads to change of law may not be public opinion, but conviction of a small number of men or even by a single individual occupying a position of commanding authority. For example, in USA, President Franklin Roosevelt carried through the legal revolution in American labour relations, symbolised by the National Labour Relations Act. This was possible due to far reaching changes in the industrial organisation and also the great depression of the early 1930s and the weakened power of the employers and the ideological strength of extreme economic individualism. When used as a tool of modernise society, law usually incorporates values which are contrary to that held by the majority. These values must be internalised. Legislation, unless accompanied by social acceptance, remains an ineffective

25. Dicey A.V., Ibid.
26. Friedmann, W., 1976, supra note 2.

instrument of social change. As an instrument of social change law involves two interrelated processes: first, institutionalisation of a new pattern of behaviour manifesting new social values; and second, internalisation of this new pattern of behaviour. Such transformation in the behaviour of the people, can in turn lead to a structural transformation of institutions as well.

Development of public opinion generally and of legislative opinion has been in England at once gradual, slow and continuous. Sometimes, the power of the legislative opinion of the day is diminished by the counter-currents or cross-currents of opinion which were not in harmony with the prevalent opinion of the time. Public debate over the abortion issue in the USA reflects this complex interaction between legal change and public opinion and also counter-currents of opinion. From the mid-1960s to the mid-1970s there was a strong parallel growth in the public acceptance of a women's right to have an abortion under certain circumstances like rape, birth defects or when the mother's health was in danger. The Supreme Court, in the famous Roe v Wade case (1973), legalised abortion all over the USA. But due to mounting pressures from the anti-abortion lobby, headed by pro-life forces and the Catholic Church, in 1977, the Supreme Court ruled that the government was not obligated to pay for abortion, even though every woman had a legal right to obtain one. Public opinion remains divided concerning the right to life and freedom of choice issues. Conflicting values over this issue often led to contradictory policy decisions. Often a well-organised and influential minority can delay changes indefinitely, although a majority of the people might favour it.

In a democratic polity, law generally follows public opinion and this opinion is rooted in the public sentiments and moral values of the people. But when law is expected to lead public opinion, it is necessary to educate the people in new values. Unless new values are internalised, people will resist change social movements. Sometimes social activists or powerful interest groups, help to mobilise public opinion in favour of new policies.

If law marches ahead of public opinion hoping the latter will fall in line with new policies and would bring about an attitudinal change, law generally remains ineffective and is not likely to achieve its goal of social engineering.

Relationship between Public Opinion and Policy Changes in the United States

Some major studies (Weissberg, 1976; Monroe, 1977; Page and Shapiro, 1983, 1992) examined the relationship between public opinion and public policy in the US over time. Weissberg concluded that depending on the topic and the time period, opinion/policy congruence does occur, however, widespread instances of incongruity can also be found.[27] For he held that public preferences could provide an intelligible guide for the formation of public policy if they were based on substantial amount of knowledge, were stable and were coherent. But this was not so in actuality. Monroe's conclusion was that the preferences of the public on most issues of any importance tend to be rather stable. For, people generally resist changing their minds. Opinions are a reflection of social factors (such as economic status, race and religion) and these inputs will generally be constant, therefore stabilising influences. There is a reinforcing effect of personal contact in everyday life. Political parties and leaders take some sort of

27. Weissberg, Robert, 1976, *Public Opinion and Popular Government*, New Jersey, USA: Prentice Hall, Inc.

positions over the years and thus influencing loyal partisans to emulate them. Individual differences largely cancel each other out and aggregate stability is generally noticed. Therefore, he concluded that there seems to be a tendency for public opinion on a major issue to move continually in the same direction. Short-term fluctuations may appear, but the trend over a number of years will usually be consistent.[28]

Page and Shapiro's study (1983, 1992) based on survey questions asked by reputed organisations like National Opinion Research Centre (NORC), General Social Survey (GSS), and Gallup Polls between 1935 and 1990 indicated that the collective policy preferences of the American public are predominantly rational, have been quite stable. Sensible opinions have developed and changed in a reasonable fashion, responding to changing circumstances and to new information. Opinion change did occur but usually modest in fashion. They admit that the United States is a pluralistic nation of many distinct social groupings and public opinion is not altogether uniform across groups. But, the parallel public partly reflect the general stability of public opinion because political information and interpretation conveyed to the public have become highly unified due to the development of centralised national mass media of communication.[29] Smith in his study has analysed that changes in aggregate public opinion are generally slow and steady, but whether slow or rapid, are largely explicable by rational factors. Measuring opinion change rests on sound and consistent measurement.[30]

---

28. Monroe, A.D., 1925, *Public Opinion in America*, New York: Dodd, Mead & Co.
29. Page, B.I. and Shapiro, R.Y., 1972, *The Rational Public, Fifty Years of Trends in Americans Policy Preferences*, Chicago: The University of Chicago Press.
30. Smith, T.W., 1994, "Is There Real Opinion Change?", *International Journal of Public Opinion Research*, Vol.6, No.2.

On the other hand, numerous authors contend that ordinary citizens have little influence over government policies. Scholars like Lowi (1969) and a host of interest group specialists (Scholzman and Tierney, 1986; Cigler and Loomis, 1986; Gais, Peterson and Walker, 1984) argue that government policies have become the domain of privileged interests in American society. Rather than reflecting mass preferences, policy making reflected an elite dominated competition between interest groups (Mills, 1956; Dahe, 1956; Schattschneider, 1960; Buchanan and Tullock, 1962). American public appears uninformed and uncertain about issues and it is difficult to make a connection between mass preferences and government policies. In the absence of a mass public connection to policies, groups and agencies with intense stakes in the outcome are seen as the major players in American politics.

Zaller has shown in his study[31] that public opinion is influenced by elites, like politicians, high-level government officials, journalists, activists, experts and policy specialists. The information that reaches the public is highly selective and stereotyped views of what has taken place. People have low information about politics and display low awareness. Shift in mass attitudes roughly coincides with the shift in elite attitudes. This perspective stresses that elites strategically manipulate public opinion for the sake of their own policy goals (Rosentone and Hansen, 1993).

Thus, congruence between policy and opinion may be achieved through democratic electoral process or by the government manipulating public preference. Whether public opinion drives policy making or is driven by the policy mak-

31. Zaller, J.R., 1992, *The Nature and Origins of Mass Opinion*, Cambridge, Massachusetts: Cambridge University Press.

ers will depend on the given issue in a given situation.

Despite the apparent downfall of the rational man in democratic theory and the rise of interest group dominance, there are documented cases when policy does fall in line with the preferences of the majority. Wright, Erikson and MacIver (1993) have shown that in state politics atleast, states with more liberal public opinion tend to have more liberal policies. Abortion politics in the states reflect this variation in public preferences as well. In USA public opinion has led to policy enactments. Even in case of abortion, public opinion has influenced policy making at the national level as well as in the state level.

Interplay between Public Opinion and Law in India

The founders of the Indian Republic were keen to establish an egalitarian society. They tried to use law as an instrument to put an end to social discrimination and create a new social order, based on equality and justice. A number of social legislations were enacted to liberate the weaker and deprived sections of the Indian society. Many of these laws promised equal rights to women and strove to remove gender discrimination. But, an unfavourable social environment and strong tradition of gender inequality prevented the realisation of the constitutional goal. Legal system is conditioned by the social system in which it evolves and operate. Anti-women bias and entrenched patriarchal interests in the Indian society not only obstructed and delayed the making of progressive laws, but also came in the way of their effective implementation.

The experience of the legislators in India illustrates that in a democracy it is not possible to impose a law on an utterly hostile community. Prime Minister Nehru had a tough time in getting the Hindu Code Bill passed in the 1950s, because the people were not ready for a radical change in the social and family system. Progressive laws as envisaged by Nehru and Ambedkar were much ahead of the community's thinking and social climate. Laws were finally enacted after much resistance from the conservative sections, and remained restricted and weak and were not even effectively enforced due to prevalence of social prejudice and patriarchal values.

However, in 1970s and 1980s, womens organisations and groups rallied effectively around issues of gender violence, rape, dowry deaths, *sati*, foeticide, etc. They demanded law reforms to check the rising tide of crime against women. In the early August of 1982, 30 women's organisations in Delhi, under the name of 'Dehaj Virodhi Chetna Manch' (Anti-Dowry Consciousness Raising Forum), jointly organised a protest march against dowry and they were joined by several hundred ordinary men and women including the parents of dowry victims. These demonstrations focussed public attention on the shortcomings of the Act, the laxity of the enforcement machinery and demanded punishment and social boycott of the dowry oppressors. Such collective efforts could no longer be ignored and the government responded by referring the Dowry Prohibition Act (DPA), 1961 to the Joint Select Committee of both the Houses of Parliament. Based on its recommendations, the Act was amended first in 1984 and later again in 1986. Activists thus mobilised public support in changing the law. Social awakening was stirred up by the growing feminist movement. This was supported by a sharp increase in the media coverage, that in turn contributed to the popular recognition of dowry harassment and violence. Building up of a strong public opinion by concerted group action thus proved more meaningful and effective than mere enactment of parliamentary statutes. The Joint Committee of Parliament, in its report of August 10, 1982, strongly expressed that the best precursor of such social reforms is in social thinking, behaviour and the creation of strong public opinion. Laws can prove effective only if they are backed by the major sections of the society. Two conditions were essential:

(1) There must be a favourable social climate in support of that law. In other words supportive public opinion must accompany the law.

(2) Administrative willingness to implement that law or else it would be a dead letter. The Constitution of India envisaged far reaching social changes through law. A number of social legislations were enacted granting wider rights to women. However, in 1950s, at the time of the Hindu Code Bill, public policy had to adjust itself accordingly, for fear of not being able to enforce law. Gradually, women's movements aroused greater social awareness and mobilised public opinion in favour of law reforms and enforcement. The need of the hour is to focus attention on changing the social attitudes in favour of gender equality. For, law promises new hope to women, but prejudices, hostile attitudes and irrational customs still hold them back. While a strong political will is a must, the community's and society's acceptance and support goes a long way to make place for the change. Sustained campaigns from women's groups especially since the 1970s paved the way for more effective legal changes.

In developing countries like India, law is expected to lead social change. Activists, lawyers and judges in India have tried to deliver justice to women through legal processes. Social legislations can play a significant role in initiating the process of social change. Law can create empowerment directly by conferring rights on the person whom it wants to empower or by imposing liabilities on other persons, towards the person to be empowered. It can cause empowerment by strengthening the institutional infrastructure for enforcing such rights and liabilities and it can cause empowerment by supporting, stimulating and monitoring the attitudinal and value change in society.[32]

Judiciary has shown increasing sensitisation to the problems faced by women especially in cases dealing with dowry related offences and dowry deaths.[33]

In the Shobha Rani vs V.M. Reddi[34] case, the Supreme Court upheld that demanding dowry amounts to cruelty and allowed the wife to get divorce on this ground.

In several dowry cases, the Supreme Court reversed the decisions of the lower courts which had acquitted the accused in dowry cases. The positive judicial response is evident in the judgment of Justice Mohan in Panniben v State of Gujarat case:[35] "Every time a case relating to dowry death comes up it causes ripples in the pool of conscience of this court. Nothing can be more barbarous, nothing could be more heinous than this sort of crime...".

Dowry offences and death occur within the safe premises of homes and it is difficult to prove domestic cruelty. The very nature of these offences requires a less technical and socially sensitive approach by various components of the criminal justice system. The Supreme Court dealt with such a

32. Sathe, S.P., 1993, *Towards Gender Justice*, Pune: Research Centre of Women's Studies, SNDT, Women's University.
33. Sarkar, L., 1987, "Women and The Law", *Annual Survey of Indian Law*, Vol. XXIII, New Delhi: Indian Law Institute.
34. AIR, 1988, SCC 121.
35. AIR, 1992, SCC 1817.

question in Stree Atyachar Virodhi Parishad v Dilip Nathumal Chordia[36], in an appeal against the decision of acquittal given by the Bombay High Court. The Supreme Court observed that it was necessary for the legal order to move forward for protection of women, and the criminal justice system to respond to the needs of the society. The investigating agency must display a live concern and the court must also display greater sensitivity to criminality and avoid on all counts "soft justice".

Through Social Action Litigation (SAL), the courts have tried to advance the cause of women, have come to the rescue of undertrial women prisoners, prevented torture and ill treatment in police lock-ups, tried to bring relief to women in protective homes and have upheld their right to free legal aid.

SAL strategies were devised to assist relatives of victims in filing private complaints and later, this was extended to women's organisations to intervene in many bride-burning cases the Sudha Goel case,[37] the Satyarani Chadha and others v State Delhi Administration,[38] the Shakuntala and others v State,[39] the Haryana Mahila Sansthan and others v Devi Lal and others.[40] By resorting to this device, women's organisations have been able to raise public consciousness, lobby for changes in the dowry law, and prevent possible manipulation by unscruplous and dishonest police officers and make the

36. 1989, (1) SCALE 330, Sivaramayya, B., "Women and the Law", 1989, XXV *Annual Survey of Indian Law*, Indian Law Institute, pp. 326-27.
37. Sudha Goel case, AIR, 1986, SC, 250.
38. Satyrani Chadha case, AIR, 1986, SC, 205.
39. Shakuntala and others v State (25), 1984, *Delhi Law Times*, 33.
40. Haryana Mahila Sansthan and Others v Devilal and Others, Criminal Writ Petition No. 931-936 of 1988.

subordinate judiciary aware of the need for taking suffering seriously and disposing of cases expeditiously.[41]

Thus, by acting as the conscience-keeper of the government, the judiciary could make law the delivery system of social justice.

But often the people and the law enforcing agencies remain passive prisoners of irrational customs and cruel practices and fail to enforce new legislations. For example, the concept of dowry has been intimately linked with ancient customs, that it has become legitimised in the minds of the people and is not perceived as immoral or illegal.[42] Hence, dowry, though legally prohibited, continues to be the general social practice in most regions and communities in India.

The legal approach of reform through law and public policy in India has not yielded very positive results. While some legal rights have been exercised, most of them have remained only on paper. Bigamy is not extinct, child marriages have not stopped, especially in villages, dowry has assumed threatening dimensions, divorce remains unacceptable in Hindu society, right to inheritance of parental property is rarely claimed by women. Crime and violence against women have increased. Malnutrition and illiteracy are alarming. Growing consumer culture has led to further devaluation and commodification of women.

Legislation appears to be an inadequate instrument when it comes to massive social regeneration, to a transformation

---

41. Jethmalani, Ram, "Dowry and the Law Subversion of Human Rights", in Gandhi P.K., (ed.), 1985, *Social Action Through Law Partnership for Social Justice*, New Delhi: Concept.
42. Jethmalani, R. and Dey, P.K., "Dowry Deaths and Access to Justice", in Jethmalani, R., (ed.) 1995, *Kali's Empowerment: Law and Dowry Deaths*, New Delhi: Haranand.

of values, attitudes and the ways people relate to their daily lives. Changes in legal mandates alone will not necessarily result in equality. Change in law must be accompanied by change in social attitudes in order to realise the ideal of gender equality. Change may be slow, but the process has begun. Enlightened public opinion is a better safeguard to ensure justice than ineffective enactments.

II

Law and Women: Feminism and Feminist Jurisprudence

Law is being used as an important instrument for transforming the status of women. The complex interaction between law and public opinion must be explored in order to understand the true impact of public policies on the position of women. Women all over the world have launched powerful movements to reverse centuries of discrimination and injustice, are mobilising against violence and oppression, are demanding equal rights, greater opportunities for development, equitable laws and control over their earnings and bodies. Feminism has become a truly global movement, shaped by and reflecting the interests of women in every region of the world. Feminism symbolises an awareness of oppression on domestic, social, economic levels, accompanied by a willingness to struggle against such subjugation. They have focussed their attention on equalising strategies, which represents attempts to improve women's access to existing education, employment, health care, credit and other opportunities, and ultimately to make resources more responsive to women's needs.[1] UNO promoted the development of international feminism and women's movements by creating national and international forums for action. The UN International Women's Year, (1975), Decade for Women (1976-85) and UN Conferences in Mexico City, Copenhagen, Nairobi and Beijing, all nourished the international connections among women in innumerable large and small ways. But much remains to be done. The UN report on women (1945-1996) clearly states that "the world's 2.8. billion women remain humanity's, largest marginalised group."[2] Although there is a formal recognition of women's right and a legal acceptance of women's equality with men, extensive data gathered by the UN show that women continue to face discrimination and marginalisation. They have less money, less education, lower status, lower self-esteem and less power. They are underrepresented in public life, almost everywhere. They are still segregated mostly in women's jobs which are low paid, face violence at workplace, at home and at public places. But the issue of women's equality is now acquiring a new significance and a dynamic feminist movement has created a ideological mandate for moving toward substantial equality between sexes.[3] How far has law been able to grant actual equality of status and opportunities to women must be examined.

---

1. Chowdhury, Nazma, Nelson, Barbara, J., et al., "Redefining Politics: Patterns of Women's Political Engagements from a Global Perspective", in Nelson, B.J. and Choudhury, N., (eds.), 1997, *Women and Politics*, New Delhi: Oxford University Press.
2. UN Report on Women,1945-1996, Paris: UNESCO.
3. Chafe, W.H., 1989, *The Paradox of Change: American Women in the Twentieth Century*, New York: Oxford University Press.

Women's Movement in the US

The history of the women's movement in the US is often described as 'two waves'. The first wave refers to the period from the Seneca Falls Convention in 1848 to passage of the nineteenth amendment granting women the right to vote in 1920. The second wave describes the developments from approximately 1960 to the present. Women's involvement in the nineteenth century abolition and twentieth century civil rights campaigns aroused feminist consciousness.

The post-Second World War period represented the turning point in the history of American women. Their increasing educational attainments and labour force participation made feminism a vigourous, dynamic and far reaching social movement. The 1960s saw the formation of a number of organisations to promote the advancement of women in economic and political roles and to preserve women's reproductive rights. The National Organisation for Women (NOW), the National Women's Political Caucus, the Abortion Rights Action League, the Women's Equity Action League, and the Women United all contributing to expansion of feminist activities. This movement embraced a multiplicity of concerns and issues from abortion rights to equal pay to the Equal Rights Amendment (ERA). Although passed by the Congress in 1972, banning discrimination on the basis of sex, ERA failed to get the ratification from the states. Opponents held that it threatened to abolish all distinctions between the sexes, subvert the family and sanction sexual deviancy. While for the proponents, the amendment represented a significant affirmation of equality as well as a means of attaining it.

The failure of the ratification device proved to be a setback but the movement emerged with impressive political organisational skills. The movement has been battling over issues likes abortion, child care, violence, pay equity, sexual harassment and aim at a broad social change and empowerment of women.

Wollstonecraft's book[4] is the classic statement of women's rights as rational human subjects. She delivered a powerful critique of the social effects of excluding women from proper education and of denying them rationality. de Beauvoir's philosophical study[5] declares that gender is not natural but constructed. "One is not born but becomes a woman." She held that women have in general been forced to occupy a secondary place in the world in relation to men. This subservient standing is imposed by strong environmental (patriarchal) forces of education and social tradition.

Friedan's book[6] explodes the myth of femininity promoted during the decade by advertisements and women's magazines. She deplored the conditioning of women from childhood to accept and pursue the role of wife and mother and depend on male superiority and called on women to dispel the cobwebs of feminine mystique and seek a move fulfilling life as human beings. Friedan's book had a direct impact on the consciousness of American women.[7]

During the past three decades, thousands of formal and

4. Wollstonescraft, Mary, 1792, *A Vindication of the Rights of Woman*, London: J.Johson, and Boston: Thomas and Andrews, (eds.), 1992, *Miriam Brody*, Harmondsworth: Penguin.
5. de Beauvoir, Simone,1949, *The Second Sex*, (trans. & ed.), Parshley, H.M., 1952, New York: Knopf.
6. Friedan, Betty, 1963, *The Feminine Mystique*, New York: Norton and London: V. Gollancz.
7. —, 1977, Editorial Research Report on the Women's Movement, Achievements and Effects, Washington D.C.: Congressional Quarterly, Inc.

informal women's groups have emerged in response to the needs and interests of women of different beliefs, races, ethnic heritages, sexual identities, classes, religions and regions. Reformist feminists believe in reform of the existing system, radicals are engaged in the battle for consciousness raising while the women of colour are trying to explore how gender and colour intersected and have begun to articulate a more socially encompassing and complex picture of woman's place in society. The feminists are increasingly influencing the public opinion in favour of women's rights. The women's movement together with changes in the economy, employment and birth control has transformed women's expectations about how they will live and work.

Women's huge influx in the workforce in the USA has been the greatest economic and social phenomena of the century. In 1950, women constituted 29 per cent of the American workforce and today the figure has risen to 46 per cent. Though women have not yet achieved pay equity, they exercise increasing economic influence. They are poised to become the dominant social, economic and political force of the next century.[8]

Feminist Theory

Feminism is both an intellectual perspective and a social movement, its theories and its practice are interwoven.[9] Historically, the thrust of feminist argument lay in its rejection of a naturally gendered psychology or social function. For liber-

---

8. Mary, C. Hickey, "How women have changed the workforce", *Ladies Home Journal*, *The Hindu*, June 25, 2000.
9. Diana, Coole, "Feminism and Politics", in Leftwich, Adrian, 1990, *New Developments in Political Science: An International Review of Achievements and Prospects*, England: Edward Elgar.

als, gendered characteristics are primarily a result of cultural pressures and of socialisation. For socialists, feminine consciousness results from experience. For essentialists experiences of women differ.

Feminists have pointed to an explicit patriarchal domination in practice. The state and its agencies are manned predominantly by men and are used to sustain male power in the private realm. The concept of patriarchy is the most distinctive and innovative contribution of feminism to political thought (Coole, 1990). It implies a system of social structures and practices in which men dominate, oppress and exploit women. For liberal feminists, such a state must be transformed while the radical feminists regard state as a patriarchal institution from which women have nothing to gain.

Different theoretical frameworks have been used by feminists to construct a vision of a more egalitarian gender system. Three identifiable groups in the women's movement committed to changing the status of women were liberal, socialist and radical.

Liberal feminism has been the best known feminine movements throughout the world. It combines a theoretical and a practical commitment to extending to women the liberal values of personal freedom and social equality, traditionally accorded to men. They draw inspiration from the liberal arguments against sexual inequality developed in the seventeenth and the nineteenth centuries by such thinkers as Mary Wollstonecraft and John Stuart Mill. They focus on extending to women the rights that men have gained in education, employment, and civic and political life. They seek a society in which no distinction is made according to gender discrimination and pursue this goal through lobbying, legislation and litigation. Thus, they demand equal rights and self determination for women within the framework of the legal system. Through public policy, public debate in the communication media and through education, they want to change old habits and institutions which undermine women and make them subservient to men.

By contrast radical feminist groups tended to be more eclectic and more interested in changing consciousness than changing laws. The socialist feminists try to locate women's subordination in the economic, social and cultural processes. They focus primarily on social relations rather than on abstract rights of the individuals. They locate the sources of women's oppression in the structure of capitalism and regarded major structural changes as necessary. They have challenged the capitalist economic and social relationship as these perpetuate gender oppression. They believed in the extricable links between race, class and gender oppressions and therefore focussed upon uniting with other oppressed groups in fighting all forms of oppression rather than organising or, struggling separately for women's rights. Radical feminists define sexual relations and sexuality as the centre of their feminist framework and argue that societies, as they are currently arranged, are patriarchal—they are run, organised and defined by men for their own benefit. They have identified men as oppressors and stressed that women and men have conflicting interests and believe that nothing but the elimination of patriarchy will ever sufficiently achieve the aims of the feminists movement. Their goal was to politicise the personal and personalise the political and to develop a woman's culture. The dichotomy between the two in conventional political thinking actually conceals the crucial interdependence of these spheres and it has been used ideologically to justify women's exclusion from public politics, and confine them to narrow domestic sphere. They seek to rediscover the lost and devalued aspects of women's culture and to create their own alternative organisation and communities.

While the liberal feminists sought moderate accommodation, the socialist and radical feminists demanded radical transformation.

Some feminists and post structuralist theorists began to criticise what they regarded as the ethnocentric assumptions of maintstream feminist theory and western social science which they maintain are inappropriate to the study of Third World people. Different cultures and societies must not be construed in universalist frameworks but must be studied in own terms. In 1980s we witness the emergence of multicultural feminism. The feminist practice and theory that developed around the globe was different in different countries because of their different histories, cultures, social structures and problems. Multicultural feminism recognise that women live in many different kinds of situations. Role of gender must be understood in its relationship to other factor like race, ethnicity, class etc. This approach recognises that women share the similarities and also experience the differences of a socially grounded womanhood. They focus on respect for differences, recognition of similarities and necessity of alliances to solve social problems. In fact, post-structuralist feminism does not reduce women's oppression to singular or universal factors but rather examines the multiple and shifting dimensions of the subordination of women.[10] Post-modern feminists seek to uncover the way in which 'reality' is constituted by language and investigate the legal, cultural and political discourses through which the identities

---

10. Kapur, Ratna and Cossman, Brenda, 1996, *Subversive Sites: Feminist Engagements with Law in India*, New Delhi: Sage.

of women are constituted. Feminism today is a worldwide movement, shaped by and reflecting the interest of women in every region of the world.

Change through Law

Liberal feminism puts an increasing emphasis on change through law and the courts. It was therefore less threatening and in some ways more effective than radical and socialist feminism.[11] They advocate reform of discriminatory laws. They argue in favour of affirmative action to create substantial equality. Law can play an important role in advancing women's equality by removing the legal obstacles that have limited women's full participation. Law, if effectively enforced, could remove gender inequality. This brings the liberal feminists close to the functional school of jurisprudence which holds that law can guide and monitor transformation of social life.

Feminist Jurisprudence

The nineteenth century marked the beginning of a feminist jurisprudence which were synonymous with the liberal philosophy of human rights. Liberal feminists stress the role of law reform in changing the position of women and ending oppression. They aim to dismantle patent inequality and gender biases in law. In the early feminist campaigns, law was seen to promote equal formal rights to women. In the formal approach, equality is seen to require equal treatment and is equated with sameness. But soon it was discovered that parity

---

11. Becker, M., Bowman, C.G. and Torrey, M., 1994, *Feminist Jurisprudence, Taking Women Seriously Cases and Materials*, American Casebook Series, Minnesota: West Publishing Co.

in formal rights did not secure parity in actual opportunity. In the middle of the 19th century there emerged the alternative strategy of making equal claims based on difference. This substantive equality approach takes into account the substantive inequality of the disadvantaged groups in society and advocates affirmative action that is special treatment. The difference model took into account the reality of women's lives and argued that law should be moulded to meet the existing needs. The focus is on the actual impact of the law.

However, in the 1970s, feminist legal scholarship began to challenge the traditional premises of liberal feminist jurisprudence. An abstract legal mandate was unlikely to lead to major social transformation. The liberal feminist perspective law was seen as an instrument of patriarchal oppression. Law was seen to be based on male norms, male experience, male domination and continues to shape and sustain unequal power relations. Feminists hold that the patriarchal system places and retains men at the top of the hierarchy and perpetuates their dominance through law. Catherine Mackinnon has propounded the dominance model, which identifies sexual exploitation as the basis of women's oppression and held that contemporary societies are based on male domination, and women are objectified by and for men. Law reflects male understanding and not women's experience. She, therefore, advocated consciousness raising as a method for challenging oppression, and women would collectively and critically redefine their experiences and produce a critical form of knowledge. Women's experience must be revealed and communicated in order to transform the form and content of law and prevailing concepts of justice and fairness.[12] Similarly,

12. Mackinnon, C.A., 1987, *Feminism: Unmodified Discourses on Life and Laws*, Cambridge, Massachusetts: Harvard University Press.

Janet Rifkin asserts that law is "a paradigm of maleness" and "the ultimate symbol of masculine authority in patriarchal society."[13] Rifkin has traced women's exclusion from the public sphere in the capitalist world, emergence of patriarchal culture, creation of property, whereby women became a form of property. Law originated for protection of men's property and mystification of this patriarchal culture which justified the subordination of women and celebration of masculine values.

Similarly, the feminists scholarship in Scandinavian countries basing their analysis on social, scientific approach claimed that women's experience must be the basis for restructuring law. For example, Tove Stand Dang (1987) advocated application of women's concept of fair and just to improve the society.[14]

Marxist feminist Zillah Eisenstein saw law as a discourse. It occupies a space between the 'real' and the 'ideal'. It operates as a political language. It articulates the 'idea' of equality without necessarily creating equality in 'real' terms.[15]

Cultural feminists seek to celebrate women's distinctiveness and hold that law should value and embody women's characteristics: nurturance, empathy and correctedness. Carol Gilligan is a leading exponent of this school. Her work, *In a Different Voice* (1982) has been proclaimed to have pioneered a revolution in psychology and social sciences. She held that women bring to the feminine experience and con-

13. Rifkin, J., 1980, "Towards a Theory of Law and Patriarchy", *Harvard Women's Law Journal*, 3: 83, 84, 87, 88, 92.
14. Smart, Carol, 1995, *Law, Crime and Sexuality: Essays in Feminism*, London: Sage.
15. Eisenstein, Zillah, R., 1988, *The Female Body and the Law*, Berkeley, Los Angeles, California: University of California Press.

struction of social reality a distinctive voice and a moral conviction which is different from the masculine mode. She calls the latter the ethics of justice, which is the basis of the legal system. This ethics of justice relies on objectivity, rationality and emotional distance. The feminine mode, which she calls "the ethics of caring", is based on connectedness, subjective emotion and responsibility for maintaining relationship. The ethics of justice is founded on the idea that everyone should be treated the same, while ethics of caring rests on the premise of non-violence, that no one should be hurt. Women care more about human relationships. They are likely to solve problems by thinking about the effects of various possible solutions on others, whereas men solve problems by reference to abstract norms. Thus, including women in decision-making institutions would result in different and more peaceful outcomes. Gilligan suggests that this is needed is a more generative view of human life in which the ethics of justice and the ethics of caring can both be deployed.[16]

Post-modern feminists investigate the legal, cultural and political discourses through which the identities of women are constituted. Mary Joe Frug, a non-essentialist, post-modern feminist, claims that law is gendered and it played a significant role in construction of identities of women.[17]

However, in constructing a new jurisprudence, feminists give a renewed legitimacy to the power of law to organise and regulate our lives. Law can both facilitate change and can be an obstacle to change too. Therefore, in the ultimate analy-

---

16. Gilligan, Carol, 1982, *In a Different Voice*, USA: Harvard University Press.
17. Greenberg, J.G., "Introduction to Postmodern Feminism", in Frug, M.J., (ed.), 1992, *Post-Modern Legal Feminism*, New York and London: Routledge.

sis, law must be seen as a site of discursive struggle.[18] It is important to sustain an emphasis on non-legal strategies and local struggles to tackle the oppression of women.[19] Rhode too asserts that, "we must appreciate both the capacities and limitations of law as an instrument of public policy."[20]

Thus, women's studies in law have travelled a long way, from the study of law as a mechanism for combating sexism to the articulation of a distinctively feminist view of law as such and a genuine theoretical endeavour to identify the core of gender-based domination. Feminist jurisprudence in its most contemporary phase offers powerful arguments to the effect that law itself is a masculine enterprise. This phase manifests an ambivalent attitude towards law. They decry the importance of the legally oriented victories which have been attained by the women's movement in the areas of equality of opportunities, in politics and employment, affirmative action, preferential treatment, etc. They are more concerned with continuing gender inequality in economic, political and social spheres and ineffectiveness of law in dealing with domestic violence, rape, employment discrimination and endless kinds of exploitation of women. Carol Smart (1995) has identified the 'maleviolence' of law, in its congruence with masculine culture, and asserts that law must be 'decentred', so that atleast one epistemological source of male domination can be by passed.[21]

---

18. Smart, Carol, 1989, *Feminism and the Power of Law*, London: Routledge.
19. Smart, C., 1986, "Feminism and Law: Some Problems of Analysis and Strategy", *International Journal of the Sociology of Law*, 14.
20. Rhode, D., 1989, *Justice and Gender*, London: Harvard University Press.
21. Cambell, Tom, D., "The Contribution of Legal Studies", in Goodwin, R.E., and Pettit, P., (eds.), 1993, *A Companion to Contemporary Political Philosophy*, USA: Blackwell.

Feminist Perception of 'Abortion' in USA

Reproductive freedom has been at the centre of feminist demands in the USA and the abortion issue has been the focus of public debate. It has raised fundamental questions relating to women's identity and their capacity to define the terms of their existence.

A feminist perspective on abortion gives high priority to the interests, claims and rights of women. The liberal feminists take into account the well-being of individual women and are concerned about the devastating impact of pregnancy and motherhood on involuntarily pregnant women. They argue that pregnancy involves a woman's relation to her own body, over which she needs control for her emotional health and her sense of identity. Hence, law should leave decision-making in this area to the individual citizens most concerned. Restrictive laws jeopardise the interest of women, are injurious to common good, increase the number of illegal, unsafe, unhygienic abortions with high risks to the women involved.

The radical feminists view law as the key mechanism for the reproduction of patriarchal oppression. Laws often work against women in the courts. Mackinnon considers the right to privacy arguments as dangerous for woman as it presupposes a fallacious distinction between matters that are in principle private and those that are public. She asserts that women got abortion as a private privilege not as a pubic right. Abortion was legalised and the government set the conditions under which women gain access to the right. Virtually, every ounce of control women won out of this legalisation has gone directly into the hands of men.[22]

---

22. Mackinnon, C.A., supra note 12.

The American society, in the opinion of Held,[23] remains "immersed in patriarchy" which focusses on the power wielded by men over women in social relations of reproduction. Men dominate political decision-making on the issue of abortion.

Abortion in the opinion of socialist feminists involves not merely the question of woman's right to privacy as stressed by the judiciary but also social roles. Unless women are able to control their child bearing capacity, they can never assume positions of full equality. By casting abortion issues solely in terms of individual autonomy, the court has obscured their collective implications, and reaffirmed the public and private dichotomy that feminism challenges. Petchesky rejected the privatisation of maternity and held that control over one's body was not merely a liberal right but a positive and necessary social condition of decent living. If women were to be compelled to carry pregnancies to term, society would have to resume full responsibility for the health and welfare of mothers and children. It is a social right—a necessary social service that society ought to make available to all women. Its accessibility is essential to all women. No category of women—poor, young, handicapped—should be excluded from reproductive freedom.[24]

Abortion poses a painful choice for women. Gilligan's (1982) interviews with women who confronted this decision reveals that women viewed their problem as centred on concern for conflicting responsibilities rather than competing rights.

Feminists also stress the asymmetrical impact of pregnancy. Since pregnancy occurs in a women's body, she has to

---

23. Held, Virgima,1982, book review, Signs 7, No.3, Spring, p.696.
24. Petchesky, R.P., 1984, *Abortion and Women's Choice: The State, Sexuality and Reproductive Freedom*, New York: Longman.

face the major consequences of conception (Maguire, 1982; Petchesky, 1982).

Right to abortion, according to Jaggar, is not absolute but contingent to the social situation in which women find themselves. In the contemporary individualistic society, mothers bear the primary responsibility for the care and development of children born, hence decisions should be made by those who are importantly affected by them.[25]

In fact, cultural feminists like Ruddick and Gilligan illuminate different ways in which men and women view moral decision in general and abortion decisions in particular. They are also suggestive of women's moral sensibilities. Moral judgements of women were closely tied to feelings of empathy and care, and responsibility for others could provide valuable moral guidance on abortion issue. Hence, feminine moral sensibility could become the foundation of an ethics of reproductive freedom. Maguire welcomes the feminisation of culture.[26] Ruddick felt that maternal thought would transform politics.[27]

Women thus need the freedom to make reproductive decisions not merely to indicate a right to be left alone, but often to strengthen their ties to others, to plan responsibilities and have a family for which they can provide to pursue pro-

25. Jaggar, Alison, "Abortion and a Women's Right to Decide", in Carol, Gould and Marx, W., Watofsky, (eds.), 1993, *Women and Philosophy Toward a Theory of Liberation*, New York: Putnam's, 1983, *Feminist, Politics and Human Nature*, Totowa, New Jersey: Rowman and Allanheld.
26. Maguirie, Daniel, 1982, "The Feminization of God and Ethics", *Christianity and Crisis*, Vol. 42, No.4, 15 March.
27. Ruddick, Sara, 1980, "Maternal Thinking", *Feminist Studies*, Vol. 6, No. 2.

fessional or work commitments made to the outside world.[28]

Thus, since 1950s, the American women's movement has made reproductive rights one of its primary objectives. It has sought to transfer control over women's fertility from individual men and male dominated institutions to individual women. Feminist perceptions reflect an awareness of women's oppression and a commitment to ending it. Chafe holds that socialist and radical feminism by advocating 'collectivist' identities was alien to American culture, while liberal feminism by advocating change within the existing framework and by focusing equal opportunity for women as individuals was more consistent with the American creed.[29]

Indian Women's Movement (IWM)

Indian women too have been continuously battling for social justice and equal rights. Three distinct phases are evident in Indian women's struggle for equality. The first phase was in the 19th century when social reformers like Raja Rammohan Roy, K.C. Sen, Ishwarchand Vidyasagar, Swami Vivekananda, Swami Dayanand and others crusaded against social evils like sati, child marriage, infanticide, oppression of widows and tried to apply rational and humanitarian criteria to these problems. The social reform movement aimed to improve the position of women within the family framework, but did not envisage woman as a an equal partner of man in the societal roles outside the family. Hence, their efforts to emancipate

---

28. Dworkin, R.M., 1994, *Life Dominion: An Argument About Abortion, Euthanasia and Individual Freedom*, New York: Vintage Books.
29. Chafe, W.H., 1989, *The Paradox of Change American Women in the Twentieth Century*, New York: Oxford University Press.

women could be only limited.[30] The second phase marked the large scale participation of women in the national movement. Under Mahatma Gandhi's clarion call, women participated in large numbers in the freedom struggle and the task of social reconstruction. The credit for emphasising the economic content of women's rights and obligations goes to Nehru. He involved women in the important task of constitution-making and was instrumental in enacting a number of progressive laws which gave a new deal to women in India. The second phase of Indian feminism was decidedly more democratic in its engagement with class and caste hierarchies as they defined gender hierarchies. Since the mid-1970s has emerged the third and a more vibrant phase of Indian women's movement, which is distinctly feminist, anti-patriarchal, and draws support from other movements for social change such as the environmental movement and the campaigns against casteism and communalism.[31] Contemporary IWM sought to understand the oppressive, hierarchical relationship between men and women and societal systems in order to introduce changes and a new society.[32]

Their emphasis is on empowering women to struggle in all areas of life—the family, work and society. Thus, the second phase of the movement was more or less state sponsored while the third was more spontaneous, collective, emotional and militant and protested against violence against women.

---

30. *Towards Equality: Report of the Committee on the Status of Women in India*, New Delhi: Government of India, 1974.
31. Nair, Janaki, 1996, *Women and Law in Colonial India*, New Delhi: Kali for Women.
32. Gandhi, N. and Shah, N., 1992, *The Issues at State, Theory and Practice in the Contemporary Womens' Movement in India*, New Delhi: Kali for Women.

IWM have generally sought transformation through legal remedies.

It is constituted by a number of organisations—urban and rural, academic and activist—draw from upper middle and lower income segments of society (with leadership stratum largely upper middle class). IWM represents a new growing force in Indian society and politics.[33]

The campaigns launched by women's organisations emphasised that if the women's situation is to change, women must come together, support each other in their common struggle, and collectively exercise pressure on the government to give them their due. The power of the state as far reaching instrument of social control cannot be denied. The Indian women's movement asserts that women are social persons to insists that the family is often the site where oppression is directly experienced and manifested. But most of all it asserts that the family is private only in appearance, that intra-family relations are in fact shaped by wider structures of society. What the movement demanded was that the state intervene on the side of women rather than on the side of the status quo. Women felt that despite their limited resources, they had succeeded in engendering new ideas of womanhood and gender relations.[34]

Social disabilities and gradual isolation from the politico-

33. Katzenstein, Mary, Fainsod, 1989, "Organising Against Violence: Strategies of the Indian Women's Movement", *Pacific Affairs*, Vol.62, No.1, Spring.

34. Palriwala, Rajni, and Agnihotri, Indu, "Tradition, the Family and the State: Politics of the Contemporary Women's Movement", in Sathyamurthy, T.V., (ed.), 1998, *Region, Religion, Caste, Gender and Culture in Contemporary India*, Vol.3, New Delhi: Oxford University Press.

ideological struggles that were shaping the nation building process led to the fragmentation of the women's movement and the women's question faded from the public arena in the post-independence period (GOI, 1974). However, the recent decades saw the resurgence of the IWM and reassertion of women's claims to participate as equals in the political and the development process. In the Third World, increasing economic liberalisation and acceleration of free market capitalism have strengthened the powers of the oppressors, and have created new instruments for hegemony. Indian women joined hands to oppose the structural adjustment programmes and the new economic policies which have adversely affected them. In the mid-1980s there was a fundamentalist onslaught on the existing rights of women, through a harking back to 'tradition' and 'culture' and stressing the women's reproductive role as their only natural and historical role and projecting them as members of one or other particular community which seeks to establish its political identity by right of birth, religion or culture.

Fundamentalism provides an ideological framework while globalisation and glorification of the market provide the operative instruments to demolish women's claim to equality, freedom and dignity as individuals.[35] Despite these challenges IWM has forged ahead in its struggle for equality and dignity.

Approaches to Women's Emancipation

The problem of emancipation of women from centuries of oppression is immense.

---

35. Agnihotri, Indu and Mazumdar, Vina, 1995, "Changing Terms of Political Discourse Women's Movement in India, 1970s-1990s", *EPW*, Vol. XXX, No.29, July 29.

Western Perspective

Issue of reform versus revolution dominated the feminist debate in the west. The reformists favoured change through reform and held that women's access to equal rights would itself transform society. However, this did not happen. Hence, more revolutionary feminists began to demand not simply equality in form but equality in fact. Law must not only be used to seek access to but must aim alteration of existing social institutions. Without a fundamental reordering of societal institutions and values, women cannot achieve true party in opportunities, economic security and social status. They must focus more attention on broader issues, on structural changes in the family and the workplace, and on strategies for fundamental reallocations in wealth and political power. However, reform and revolution are not really incompatible. One has to start with reformist politics and go on the road to revolution.

The third option prescribes 'androgyny' or role sharing, both in domestic and public life. While the long-term solution is to draw men and women into domestic role sharing and enable women to compete more successfully in the public sphere.[36]

The Indian Perspective

Three basic approaches have emerged to the women's question in India. The first is the social reform approach as reflected in the 19th century social reform movement which had its roots in the English liberal philosophy. Second is the

36. Randall, Vicky, 1987, *Women and Politics: An International Perspective*, Chicago: The University of Chicago Press.

socialist approach which focusses on women's problems as part of the general problem of class exploitation. Marxists held that once women entered productive processes in large numbers, the women's question would be automatically solved. The exploitation of women by men is the focus of the third approach of the Indian feminists.[37]

The nineteenth century social reformers spearheaded the great intellectual awakening in modern India. Swami Vivekananda and Swami Dayananda, drawing from the indigenous sources, asserted the intrinsic equality of human beings and denounced the prevailing social discriminations and inequalities.

The widening social consciousness ultimately led to the emergence of Indian nationalism, intensified greatly by colonial exploitation and plunder of the Indian economy by the British. There emerged two viewpoints. Some like Ranade advocated social reform as a necessary part of the national movement, but extremists like Tilak gave precedence to political freedom which would take care of social reform once it was achieved. Gandhiji's emergence on the Indian scene and his vision of the women's role and place in society added an entirely new dimension to Indian awakening. He declared emphatically that fight for swaraj and social reform must proceed together and transformed the struggle for freedom into a mass movement by enlisting the participation of all people, including the downtrodden, the poor, the socially suppressed and also the women.

Gandhiji was able to motivate the Indian women to come

---

37. Haksar, Nandita, 1981, "Women's Problems: Three Approaches", *Mainstream*, Annual Number.

out of their homes and participate in large numbers in the 'satyagraha' and 'swadeshi' movements. He was uncompromising in the matters of women's rights. He denounced any kind of discrimination against them and advocated perfect equality between a son and a daughter in the family. He forbade child marriage and enforced widowhood, condemned dowry, and favoured simplification of marriage rites. He spoke of equality between men and women and convinced women that they were not mere 'playthings' but creative individuals and possessed qualities and attributes which were essential for the society. He inspired the Indian women to participate in politics as honourable comrades and generated self-confidence in them. He sought their total emancipation through education and helped them to break the shackles of domesticity. Women's large-scale participation in the national struggle assured them of a ready and abiding place in India's new resurgent life. Gandhiji believed in the complementary roles of men and women. Gandhiji had great faith in the nobler qualities of women like courage, perseverance, patience, humility and faith. By involving women into the political process he wanted to spiritualise politics. Feminisation of political culture could emerge as an alternative to patriarchal, male and muscle dominated competitive politics.

Dr. Ambedkar, widely proclaimed as the "father of the Indian Constitution", was also a great crusader for women's rights. He was deeply distressed by injustice inflicted on women and sought to seek their deliverance from the iniquitous injunctions laid down by the *Manusmriti.* He tried to raise their status through legal measures. It was mainly due to his painstaking work as the first Law Minister that the massive Hindu Code Bill was drafted, granting equal rights to women. "The bills was only aimed at removing the obstruction of law in the social advancement of women," remarked

Dr. Ambedkar. But, the dropping of the bill subsequently led to his resignation from the cabinet.[38]

Following these two great proponents of women's equality, framers of the Indian Constitution sought change through law and committed themselves to gender justice by granting equal rights to women. They strove to undertake the task of social engineering in order to create a just social order.

The western feminists base their perspective on their own experience. They have questioned the unequal power relations existing within a society. They stressed the need to do away with patriarchal framework where women were dominated and oppressed by men. The entire world is now talking of 'empowerment' of women within a developmental framework. Women were to become active participants in the development process and active agents of social change and not remain mere recipients of social opportunities. However, economic liberalisation along with the structural adjustment programme have worsened the economic condition of women and widened gender disparities. Women continue to be confined to low paid jobs. Globalisation has led to feminisation of labour, often at low wages and under poor conditions. Their participation in the workforce is increasing, but their share of unpaid work has not been reduced. Globalisation has also aggravated crime against women.

The 'empowerment' concept is implicitly based on the assumption of gender conflict. But man and woman do not confront each other as competitors or antagonists. Complete separation between the two sexes as advocated by radical

38. Kuber, W.N., 1979, *Dr. Ambedkar: A Critical Study*, New Delhi: People's Publishing House.

feminists is not the answer. What is required is more cementing and integrating concepts that emphasise caring and sharing, more complementary, cooperative, compatible, harmonious and egalitarian relationships that would generate dignified coexistence of both the genders.[39]

Cooperation not confrontation between men and women is the answer. Attitudinal change is needed both in men and women. Men cannot realise their full potential as long as women are prevented from achieving theirs. Men and women working together in all aspects of the political and economic realms of human existence can result in a harmonious, nonrepressive society and a better world in the future.

Women's question is really a human question. By devaluing women, men are not only dehumanising one half of the human race but actually alienating themselves. Human question involves integral concepts like human development and human rights. Human rights implies freedom from discrimination, fear, injustice, humiliation, exploitation and freedom to decent life and work. Development implies growth with equity. Human equality would mean elimination of all man-made inequalities based on gender, caste, community, race, religion, etc. Instead of a feminine perspective, a broader gender perspective is what is needed, which could cover human question and take into account the needs and interest of both the genders and integrate them to work for human betterment. Such a model of complementary roles and harmonious coexistence would provide a saner and a better paradigm than the western feminist approach, rooted in gender conflict, male supremacy and female oppression.

---

39. Haider, Saraswati, 1997, "National Policy for Women in India 1996: A Critique," *Social Scientist*, Vol.25, Nos.3-4, March-April.

Feminist Perception of Law in India

Law has been upheld as a significant instrument of social change in India. Social reformers in the 19th century, women in the independence movement, and activists in the contemporary women's movement, all have fought for women's rights and law reform. All placed faith in law's ability to deliver social change.

Social reformers sought to enact protective legislations to prohibit evil perpetrated on women. But, their discourse was heavily embedded within familialism. The second phase of women's movement stressed more on political participation of women. Their involvement in the freedom struggle and the process of constitution-making empowered them.

However, in the immediate post-independent period, the campaign for both the constitutional rights and Hindu Code Bill came to focus on formal equality. Women were easily allowed to enter public sphere but when it came to equality in the private sphere there was a storm of resistance from the traditionalist forces.

Liberal feminists consider law as an instrument of social change and reform. Through affirmative action, women could be given equal rights. While radical feminists highlight the role of law as an instrument of oppression in the patriarchal Indian social system, the contemporary women's movement continues to fight for law reforms and substantial equality. Legislative victories have been won but women continue to suffer oppression and law continues to shape and sustain unequal power relations. Feminist legal studies, a relatively new and emerging field in India, have begun to understand the role that law has played in women's oppression and to the potential role that it can play in challenging that oppression. Role of law could not actually be captured by a dichotomous understanding of law as either an instrument of oppression or of change. It is necessary to understand law and also analyse its contradictory nature in women's struggle for social change.[40]

Feminist historians have played a leading role in the articulation of a more complex understanding of the role of law in social change. Tanika Sarkar, Lata Mani, Janaki Nair and Prem Choudhury have critically examined the complex relationship between law in colonial India and women's subordination.[41] More recently, economist Bina Agarwal's study[42] of women and land rights in South Asia has provided an insightful analysis of both the importance and limitations of law and land rights, in particular for women. Archana Parashar, in her study[43] of family law reform, focusses on both the limitations and possibilities of law and holds that

---

40. Kapur, R. and Cossman, B., supra note 10.
41. Sarkar, Tanika, 1993, "Rhetoric Against Age of Consent: Resisting Colonial Reason and Death of a Child Wife", *Economic and Political Weekly*, 4 September.

    Mani, Lata, "Contentious Traditions: The Debate on Sati in Colonial India", in Sangari, K. and Vaid, S., (eds.), 1989, *Recasting Women: Essays in Indian Colonial History*, New Delhi: Kali for Women.

    Nair, Janaki, 1996, *Women and Law in Colonial India: A Social History*, New Delhi: Kali for Women.

    Choudhury, Prem, 1993, "Conjugality, Law and State: Inheritance Rights as Pivot of Control in Northern India," *National Law School Journal*.

    —, 1994, *The Veiled Women: Shifting Gender Equations in Rural Haryana*, 1880-1990, New Delhi: Oxford University Press.
42. Agrawal, Bina, 1994, *A Field of One's Own: Gender and Land Rights in South Asia*, Cambridge: Cambridge University Press.
43. Parashar, Archana, 1992, *Women and Family Law Reform in India*, New Delhi: Sage.

law can serve a 'symbolic' purpose. Symbolic legislation can be of liberating value as it can provide a focus around which forces of change can mobilise. Flavia Agnes' work[44] attempt to bring out some of the contradictions in the role of law while making concrete suggestions of how law could be made to better empower women. Hence, it is necessary to understand law as a discourse and as a site of discursive struggle over the identity and status of women.

The new scholarship has thus begun to explore the diversity of oppression that women experience, across not only class lines, but also caste, religion, ethnicity and culture and the way in which the law has been implicated in that oppression.

Feminists of the Third World countries are critical of the essentialist nature of feminist scholarship which emerged in North America. They feel it was over determined by gender and based on the experiences only of the white women and tended to ignore the plurality of women's lives and experiences based on race, religion, ethnicity and culture in different parts of the world. While the differences between men and women are significant, so are the differences among women. To define one particular group of women as representing the essence of women does violate and constraint the lives of those women who differ.

Vasuki Nesiah[45], in her critique of American legal theory,

---

44. Agnes, Flavia, 1992, "Protecting Women Against Violence: Review of a Decade of Legislation, 1980-1989," EPW, 25 April, WS-19.
45. Nesiah, Vasuki, "Towards a Feminist Internationality: A Critique of US Feminist Legal Scholarship", in Kapur, R., (ed.), 1996, *Feminist Terrains in Legal Domains: Interdisciplinary Essays on Women and Law in India*, New Delhi: Kali for Women.

has argued that they have been largely oblivious to the question of global contradictions and the impact of these contradictions on women located in developing countries. Feminists cannot involve 'women' without addressing to the specific politics and conditions of struggle through which they are socially constructed. American feminists often effect homogenisation by situating women against universalised male oppression, thus abstracting them out of their communities.

In the opinion of Archana Parashar, legal feminists seek to achieve parity between men and women. The category women is an important analytical device but must be realistically constructed in order to reflect the plurality of womens lives and experiences based on race, religion, ethnicity and culture in different parts of the world. Therefore, the identification of the most pressing problems and the choice of strategies for change are also likely to be different for different women. Hence, legal feminism must become truly plural and equally recognised concerns of all women. Knowledge thus generated must be able to transform law into better law. Parashar has stressed the need to focus on the purpose of engaging in feminist jurisprudence which is to transform society and achieve social justice for all women. Western legal feminists must acknowledge their responsibility to theorise in a sensitive and inclusive manner to understand the experience of women in the developing world.[46]

Despite the prediction of some legal theorists, law continues to govern, mould and regulate our lives. It is the distinctive way in which law operates as a terrain of political and discursive struggle that must be the focus of feminist legal

46. Parashar, Archana, "Essentialism or Pluralism: The Future of Legal Feminism" in Kapur, R., (ed.), Ibid.

studies. It is essential to take into account the broader social and economic structures in which the legal discourse is embedded.[47]

The familial ideology continues to shape Indian women's destiny. The family is a site of diverse and often contradictory experiences for women. It glorifies women as wives and mothers, as economically dependent, as passive, dutiful and self-sacrificing. Women's position in the family is one of dependence and her role is seriously undervalued.

Gender injustice, according to Nandita Haksar, is built into our legal system, it permeates and works through the minds of biased and conservative judges, brutalised policemen and commercial advocates.[48] Similarly, Lina Gonsalves' study[49] focusses on the need to eliminate the patriarchal biases affecting the implementation of laws. Legislations by themselves provide no solution to bastions of patriarchy and male domination.[50] Justice Chinappa Reddy had aptly observed that "the world today is a man's world, where a woman is never a woman in her own right, but where she is first the daughter, next the wife and last the mother of a man". He stressed the urgent need for the comprehensive revision of all laws where women are discriminated, where women need protection or where they need advancement.[51] Indian society is dominated by patriarchal values which as-

---

47. Kapur, R. and Cossman, Brenda, supra note 10.
48. Haksar, Nandita, "Dominance, Suppression and the Law", in Sarkar, L., and Sivaramayya, B., (eds.), 1994, *Women and Law*, New Delhi: Vikas.
49. Gonslaves, Lina, 1993, *Women and Law*, New Delhi: Lancer.
50. Sarkar, Lotika and Sivaramayya, B., (eds.), 1994, op.cit.
51. —, 1988, Sixth J.P. Memorial Lecture, CWDS, New Delhi, March 2.

serted that a women's first duty was to worship her husband as God, no matter how cruel, unfaithful or immoral he may be.[52] Motherhood and the ideal of a faithful, loyal, self-sacrificing wife continue to be projected through the media and the education system. The reality of subordinate position of women in India is indicated through adverse sex ratio of girls, the growing domestic violence, increasing number of dowry deaths and rape cases.[53]

Thus, contemporary feminists assert that law continues to support a patriarchal family structure, denies women an independent means of income and maintenance and subjects her to dual standards of morality.

Feminist Perception of Dowry

Ancient custom is rooted in the patriarchal family structure based on the objectification and subordination of women. Marriage in India is a sacrament, a sacred bond between two families, an institution controlling the sexuality of women. The concept of '*kanyadaan*' reduces the status of a daughter to a piece of object to be donated at the father's or the guardian's will. In marriage, emphasis is placed on the preservation of family status and honour. Therefore, the parents are keen to keep the marriage intact even at the cost of the harassment of the bride often resulting in death.

The custom of dowry is embedded in the familial ideology of patriarchy. It condemns women to an inferior sex and

---

52. Altekar, A.S., 1983, *The Position of Women in Hindu Civilisation*, Varanasi: Motilal Banarsidas.
53. Desai, N. and Krishnaraj, M., 1987, *Women and Society in India*, New Delhi: Ajanta, supra note 41; Kishwar, M., 1984, *In Search of Answers: The Indian Women's Voices From Manushi*, London: Zed Books.

makes her believe in it and confines her to the functions of child bearing, child rearing and homekeeping.[54] Thus, dowry functions as a part of the cultural system wherein the woman is a devalued object, a liability to be disposed of at a discount in the interfamily transaction that is marriage. Dowry is like a compensation to the son-in-law to keep the girl who after the an age is totally unwanted in her parent's home.[55]

Dowry is rooted in the unequal power relations between men and women. Hindu laws of property and ownership of the means of production give women negligible rights as independent entities to family income, assets and property. Thus, a woman's bargaining power vis-a-vis her husband is weak. A woman's economic independence and the lack of equal property rights force her to remain in the matrimonial home and meet the unreasonable demands of the husband and in-laws in order to preserve her marriage.

Dowry must be viewed in the larger context of women's subordination in the Indian society, her general devaluation in the Indian culture, and her economic dependence, in fact her total powerlessness and resourcelessness. The caste stratified ancient Indian society led to patriarchy and establishment of private property. Women's sexuality was increasingly controlled and their independent economic role diminished. Emerging socio-economic pattern witnessed the growing exclusion of the woman from the property of her natal family and its inheritance.[56]

54. Haksar, N. and Singh, A., 1986, *The Demystification of Law for Women*, New Delhi: Lancer Press.
55. Kishwar, Madhu, 1989, "Towards More Just Norms for Marriage: Continuing the Dowry Debate", *Manushi*, No.58.
56. Sheel, Ranjana, 1999, *The Political Economy of Dowry: Institutionalisation and Expansion in North India*, New Delhi: Manohar.

Dowry illustrates the interlocking relationships between gender, ideology, socio-economic structures and the patriarchal state.

Removal of Dowry through Law

Dowry has always been regarded as an ancient practice. The social reformers and the constitution framers never really questioned the inequality and injustice embedded in this tradition. Dowry was not regarded as an evil till it was extorted. In fact, legislators were not opposed to the idea of dowry in form of gifts. It was considered as providing security and protection to the daughter. Dowry was thus legitimised in the Indian psyche.

Law merely tried to regulate dowry and keep it within reasonable limits. The role of law in combating the evil of dowry has been ambivalent. The law reforms dealing with dowry and dowry violence were not connected to the structural inequality of women, within the family. Dowry laws not only fail to address to women's economic dependency within the family, but also in its failure to displace the dominant familial ideology which creates and substains this ideology.[57]

Judicial approach is influenced by the familial ideology and limits attempts to challenge laws that discriminate against women. The judicial approach to sex discrimination is influenced by a formal approach to equality, based on 'sameness' and often a protectionist approach to gender difference viewing women as weak and in need of protection. In some cases, courts adopt a corrective approach recommendating preferential treatment in order to compensate for past

57. Kapur, R. and Cossman, B., (eds.), 1996, supra note 10.

discrimination. Law thus operates to reinforce the familial ideology.[58]

Indian policy-makers opted for a slow and a gradual change through law while the contemporary feminists have tried to arouse public consciousness against the atrocities of dowry and focus public attention on oppression of women. They mobilised and exerted pressure on the government to strengthen the laws and ensure their better enforcement.

Both in USA and India, efforts were made to grant equality to women through law and the legal process. In the USA law has followed public opinion, it proceeded slowly in tune with change in public opinion which is slow and gradual. Unless law is accompanied by change in values it fails to bring about the much needed change.

Simone de Beauvoir[59] has shown that even when women's rights were largely recognised, long standing customs prevented their full expression. W.H. Chafe[60] has also documented that social change must be preceded by change in values and beliefs. But attitudes, especially those involving emotional matters as race or sex almost never change except under compulsion. For example, in the 1940s and 1950s, a large number of American women joined the labour force, won legal rights, yet the traditional belief that woman were primarily homemakers remained largely unchanged. Struc-

58. Cossman, B., and Kapur, R., "Women, Familial Ideology and the Constitution: Challenging Equality Rights", Kapur, R., (ed.), 1996, *Feminist Terrains in Legal Domains*, New Delhi: Kali for Women.
59. de Beauvoir, Simone, 1949, *The Second Sex*, (trans. and ed.), Parshley, H.M., London: Pan Books.
60. Chafe, W.H., 1989, *The Paradox of Change: American Women in the Twentieth Century*, New York: Oxford University Press.

tural barriers to gender equality remained and women remained clustered in all the lowest paying jobs. However, the dynamic women's movement in the 1960s and 1970s played a pivotal role in altering the mindsets of an entire generation of young women. Public opinion is rooted in social attitudes which change slowly and gradually. Sometimes, social movement led by activists groups may help to change the public opinion.

In India, on the other hand, law was ahead of public opinion and was expected to lead the process of social change. But special legislations succeeded in granting merely formal equality to women. In fact, enactment of progressive laws faced stormy resistance from different sections of people immersed in conservative values and customs. Although dowry was prohibited by law, it could be uprooted as it lay deeply embedded in the nation's psyche. Hence, law must be backed by public opinion. Change in public opinion must precede change in law, only then can law become an effective instrument of social change.

Thus, legislation alone cannot uproot deep-rooted social practices. Ancient customs have social sanctions, hence social awakening is needed against such oppressive tradition. It is essential to motivate and mobilise public opinion in favour of laws for women. Society's acceptance and support facilitates attitudinal change. Attitude within the family must change first. Parents must give equal treatment to their son and daughter, stop being partial to the son and vindictive or negligent towards the daughter. Women must shed their superstitions and ritualistic attitudes and become rational in their outlook, in fact revolt against oppressive customs. As they assume creative and independent roles, social acceptance will grow. The need of the hour is to focus attention on changing the social attitudes in favour of gender equality, for law can only create an opinion but it cannot transform people.

III

■ ■ ■

Abortion in the US: Interplay between Public Opinion and Law

From the mid-1960s onwards, feminist pressures led to abortion law reforms in the USA. Feminists came to recognise its importance for women's individual freedom of choice and effective participation in the public sphere. The issue of free choice in abortion appears to involve questions of fundamental role change for women. But, the issue has generated intense moral, ethical, religious, ideological, legal and political debates in America. "No single issue has retained such a pivotal place in our political psyche since the Vietnam war", holds Mathew E. Wetstein.[1]

Public attention to abortion came first over the question of foetal deformity. When thalidomide, an antidepressant drug caused grave deformity of foetuses, demands for abortion arose. An epidemic of rubella (German measles)

1. Wetstein, M.E., 1996, *Abortion Rates in the US: The Influence of Opinion and Policy*, Albany: State University of New York Press.

followed soon after, further dramatising the tragic implications of the ban on legal abortions. Capitalising on public sympathies for women who terminated abnormal pregnancies and for the doctors who provided illegal assistance, feminists increased their lobbying and litigation campaigns against restrictive abortion laws (refer to Appendix I for evidence that public opinion had changed in favour of legalising abortion).

Changes in public sentiments were apparent both in state legislative initiatives and in national opinion surveys. Reform bills began to surface in 1961, usually modelled on an American Law Institute proposal that allowed abortion in certain compelling circumstances. In the five years preceding, the Supreme Court's 1973 landmark abortion decision, Roe v Wade case, one-third of the states had liberalised their statutes. However, on the eve of that decision, half the states still prohibited termination of pregnancy except where necessary to preserve maternal life, even though substantial evidence indicated that such restrictive statutes were out of step with public opinion.[2] Much of the change in public opinion about abortion seems, to have resulted, ultimately, from objective material factors changes in the social and economic environment and changes in technology that preceded action by politicians or organised political groups.

In 1973, the US Supreme Court invalidated virtually every state law designed to restrict women's access to legal abortion. In Roe v Wade (1973) and its companion case, Doe v Bolton (1973), the court by a 7 to 2 margin held that women have a constitutionally protected right to legal abortion. The court asserted that women had a fundamental right

---

2. Tatalovich, Raymond and Daynes, Byron, W., 1981, *The Politics of Abortion: A Study of Community Conflict in Public Policy Making*, New York: Praeger.

of privacy to decide whether or not to bear a child. It established three things. First, it reaffirmed a pregnant woman's constitutional right of procreative autonomy, holding that, "the right of privacy is broad enough to encompass a woman's decision whether or not to terminate her pregnancy". Second, it recognised that states nevertheless do have a legitimate interest in regulating abortion. Third, it constructed a detailed regime for balancing that right and that interest. It declared roughly, that states may not forbid abortion for any reason in the first trimester of pregnancy, that they may regulate abortion in the second trimester only out of concern for the health of the mother, and finally that they may outlaw abortion altogether when the foetus has become a viable being, that is, in the third trimester of pregnancy.[3]

Although responding specifically to the laws of Texas and Georgia, the broad scope of the court's constitutional interpretation invalidated the abortion laws of almost every state and the district of Columbia. (Alaska, Hawai, New York and Washington had previously liberalised their laws. The constitutional requirements set forth in the Roe and Doe cases were basically, although not completely, met by these state laws).

Roe v Wade was a test case for the times and registered an ongoing political struggle by women for equal rights and self determination. Human reproduction is not simply a physiological process but a social process, governed by culture. Ideological norms and institutional practices pertaining to reproduction, play a central part in defining women's status, the dignity they are accorded and the degradations to which they are subjected and the degree of autonomy they are al-

---

3. Dworkin, R.M., 1994, *Lifes' Dominion: An Argument about Abortion, Euthansia and Individual Freedom*, New York: Vintage Books.

lowed or dependency they must suffer.[4]

American Public Opinion about Abortion

Much of the reason for the growth in major organised support for abortion law reform may have come from changes in American public opinion. By the eve of the court's decisions in 1973, public opinion had dramatically shifted from opposition to abortion in most cases to substantial support. "The future of the abortion issue may, in large part, be decided in the court of public opinion."[5]

The period between 1965 and 1972 were marked by the apparent liberalisation of opinions on abortion in the US.[6] In the decades that have followed the Supreme Court ruling in 1973, opinion on abortion has remained remarkably stable.[7]

Looking at the 1960s, as a whole, Blake found a decline in disapproval of economic justifications for abortion. She noted that opinion on discretionary abortion were "changing rapidly over time", and polls were recording "rapidly growing support". Relying on Gallup data, Blake found that support for elective abortion increased approximately two

---

4. Siegel, Reva, 1992, "Reasoning from the Body: A Historical Perspective on Abortion Regulation and Questions of Equal Protection," *Stanford Law Review*, 44: 261.
5. Cook, Elizabeth Adell, Ted G., Jelen, Clyde, Wilcox, 1992, *Between Two Absolutes: Public Opinion and the Politics of Abortion*, USA: Westview Press.
6. Rossi, Alice S. and Sitaraman, Bhavani, 1988, "Abortion in context Historical Trends and Future Changes", *Family Planning Perspectives*, Vol.20, No.6, November/December.
7. Page, Benjamin T. and Shapiro, Robert Y., 1992, *The Rational Public Fifty Years of Trends in American Policy Preferences*, Chicago: University of Chicago Press; Gallup Report, No.281, February, 1989.

and a half times from 1968 to 1972.[8]

Granbergs' (1980) study[9] focussing on 1965-1980, based their analysis on the data from the National Opinion Research Centre (NORC), National Fertility Surveys (NFS) and surveys done by the Centre for Political Studies (CPS). They discovered that the approval for legal abortions increased dramatically among Americans between 1965 and 1973 (from an average of 41 per cent for six different reasons in 1965 to 68 per cent in 1973). They have shown that there was a large shift between 1965 and 1970 and between 1970 and 1975. Between 1975 and 1980 there was virtually no change in approval of abortion. Thus, Supreme Court's key decision in Roe v Wade (1973) had little or no effect on public opinion.

In fact, American public opinion in 1972 preferred a more permissive situation than that which prevailed in most states at that time. Thus, change in public opinion preceded and led to the Supreme Court's key decision in the Roe v Wade case legalising abortion.

William Ray Arney and William Hyreschers Trescher's study (1976) documented a growing consensus among all Americans that "the right of a woman to have an abortion

---

8. Blake, Judith,1971, "Abortion and Public Opinion: The 1960-1970 Decade", *Science* 171, 12:540-49.

   Blake, Judith and Jorge, H., del Pinal, "Predicting Polar Attitudes Toward Abortion in the US", in J.T. Burtchaell, (ed.), 1980, *Abortion Parley*, Kansas City, KS: Andrews and McMeel.

9. Granberg, Donald, and Granberg, Berth Wellman, 1980, "Abortion Attitudes 1965-1980: Trends and Determinants", *Family Planning Perspectives*, Vol.12, No.5.

   Granberg, D. and Granberg, B.W., "Social Bases of Support and Opposition to Legalised Abortion", in Sachdev, Paul, (ed.), 1985, *Perspective on Abortion*, New Jersey: The Sacrecrow Press.

should be left entirely up to the woman and her doctor". Attitudes toward abortion have been divided into 'hard' and 'soft' reasons. 'Hard' reasons involve the physical welfare of the mother and child, whereas 'soft' reasons involve the social welfare of the mother and child. Several studies documents approval levels for abortion for physical reasons which are nearly twice as high as those for social reasons (Arney and Trescher, 1976; Barnartt and Harris, 1982; Granberg and Granberg, 1980).[10]

Rose, Ebaugh and Haney, basing their analysis on the NORC 1972-1980 data, confirmed the necessity of specifying conditions for abortion since attitudes vary greatly depending on the situation. Three-fourth or more of the respondents favour abortion for the three hard reasons while less than one-half are favourable when soft reasons exist. Their findings indicated a crystallisation of opinions regarding legalised abortion after the 1973 Supreme Court decision. "Our data, therefore, support the position that the law not only reflects public sentiment but can be effective in influencing attitudes and moral decisions."[11]

Almost every year since 1972, the National Opinion Research Centre (NORC) at the University of Chicago has

---

10. Arney, William Ray and Tescher, William, H., 1976, "Trends in Attitudes Towards Abortion, 1972-75", *Family Planning Perspectives*, Vol.8, No.3, May-June.

    —, 1982, Barnartt, Sharon, N. and Harris, Richard, J., "Recent Changes in Predictors of Abortion Attitudes", *Sociology and Social Research*, Vol. 66, April.

    —, 1980, Grangberg, D. and Grangberg, B.W., supra note 9.

11. Rose, Helen, Ebaugh, Fuchs, and Haney, Allen, C., "Abortion Attitudes in the United States: Continuities and Discontinuities," Sachdev, P., (ed.), 1985, *Perspectives on Abortion*, New Jersey: The Sacrecrow Press.

conducted a national survey of social and political attitudes. The General Social Survey (GSS) has included a battery of six questions measuring support for legal abortion. These items ask respondents whether they believe that it should be possible for a pregnant woman to obtain a legal abortion:

— if there is a strong chance of serious defect in the baby.

— if she is married and does not want more children.

— if the woman's own health is seriously endangered by the pregnancy.

— if the family has a very low income and cannot afford any more children.

— if she became pregnant as a result of rape.

— if she is not married and does not want to marry the man.

From the data gathered by NORC, GSS over the years between 1972 and 1987 demonstrate that there is a core group of about 10 per cent within the American public that would prohibit abortion for any reason. However, a third of the American people supported the right to an abortion for all six circumstances. In between those two extremes are the majority of Americans (about 60 per cent) who have consistently endorsed the view that abortion should be legal only under certain circumstances.

According to the Gallup Poll[12] conducted in September 1988, 57 per cent now favour legal abortion only under certain circumstances, while 24 per cent back unlimited access, and 17 per cent an outright ban. Since 1972, public opinion on abortion has been remarkably stable. The public has generally moved toward a position of consensus regarding

12. Gallup Report No. 281, February 1989.

abortion for health reasons, while over half of the American public still opposes abortion in the discretionary situations.

According to the Gallup Polls conducted between 1988 and 1991 public support for maintaining the legal status quo on abortion is at its highest level in three years. Nearly two-third (64 per cent) of Americans opposed an overturn of Roe v Wade decision of the Supreme Court. Craig and O'Brien[13] held that from 1965 to 1973, support for abortion grew in one-third of the states which liberalised abortion laws. In the first year following Roe, support for abortion continued upwards slightly, then levelled off, until the 1980s, when support dipped slightly. By 1990 the dip was reversed and some analysts believed the trend was to a slow growth in support for abortion in all cases. Thus, the overall support for the legality of abortion in US would remain firm, but the differences in attitudes between 'hard' and 'soft' reasons would remain wide. American public remains strongly supportive of abortion when the woman's health is endangered by continuing the pregnancy, when there is a strong chance of a serious foetal defect, and when the pregnancy is the result of rape or incest. The public is more divided when abortion is sought for economic reasons, by single unmarried women unwilling to marry, and by married women who do not want more children.

Public Opinion and Public Policy

Several empirical research (Monroe, 1979; Page and Shapiro, 1983, 1992; Wright, Erickson and MacIver, 1987) corroborate a linkage between public preferences and public policy.

13. Craig, Barbara Hinkson and O'Brien, David M., 1993, *Abortion and American Politics*, Chatham, New Jersey: Chatham House Publishers, Inc.

Liberalisation of abortion attitudes in the US appears to have been accompanied by a wave of policy enactments.

Most Americans dislike the idea of abortion, considering it a painful last resort, but most have come to accept the idea of permitting it under a variety of circumstances.

Wright, Erikson and MacIver's study[14] (1987) documented that abortion politics in the states reflect the ideological dispositions of the people. Simply the more conservative the opinion of the people in the state, the more conservative the policies of the state and vice versa. Goggin and Kim (1992)[15] showed that state abortion policy does follow state public preferences, although the effect of abortion opinion is mediated by the preferences of the state political actors that make the abortion policies, namely, governors and legislators.

Goggin and Wlezien research (1992)[16] of national abortion opinion during the 1980s indicate that the public became increasingly more supportive of keeping abortion legal "as it is now" in response to court cases and Supreme Court nominations and confirmations that challenged the abortion status quo. They became less supportive of further restrictions on the availability of abortion at a national level.

---

14. Wright, G.C., Erikson, R.S. and MacIver, J.P., 1987, "Public Opinion and Policy Liberalism in the American States", *American Journal of Political Science*, Vol.31, No.4, November.
15. Goggin, M.L. and Kim, J.K., 1992, "Interest groups, Public Opinion and Abortion Policy in the American States", paper presented at the annual meeting of the Western Political Science Association, San Francisco.
16. Goggin, M.L. and Wlezien, C., 1991, "Interest Groups and the Socialisation of Conflict", paper presented at the annual meeting of the Midwest Political Science Association, Chicago.

Supreme Court decisions (Webster, 1989; Casey, 1992) have shifted the abortion issue to the states. Empirical research has shown that restrictiveness of state abortion policy follow state abortion opinion.

Court and the Public Opinion

The court's decision of 1973 precipitated a nation wide change in the legal status of abortion. The court's decisions regarding abortion represents an effort to effect social change through the exercise of judicial review.

Did the Supreme Court decision in the Roe v Wade case in 1973 play a major part in liberalising public attitudes on the subject? Public opinion surveys made before the decision shown that public opinion had already become favourable toward legal abortion. Perhaps, the Supreme Court was reflecting social change rather than legislating it.

A sophisticated analysis by Franklin and Kosaki (1989)[17] indicates that the court in fact produced a very small rise in support for abortion in the three most clearly health related circumstances, however the public became more polarised over 'discretionary' abortions. The net direct impact of the court decision upon collective public opinion as a whole was negligible.

In the months and years since the Roe decision was handed down, there has been increased levels of debate, group mobilisation, and political action (Luker, 1984). These activities in turn have influenced citizens' preferences as well. Moreover, only a small portion of the public is aware of most

---

17. Franklin, Charles H., Kosaki, Liani C., 1989, "Republican School Master: The US Supreme Court, Public Opinion, and Abortion", *American Political Science Review*, Vol.83, No.3, September.

court decisions, and an even smaller proportion is accurately informed about them (Kessel, 1966; Murphy and Tanen Laus, 1969) On the basis of Gallup Poll in April 1975, Judith Blake found that "less than half of American adult respondents were informed about the 1973 decisions."[18] By 1983, almost a decade after the decisions, little had changed.

Rosenberg in his study concludes that in the area of public opinion, abortion, and women's rights, while there were major changes, they pre-dated court action. In fact, the Second World War had radically transformed the economic outlook of women (Chafe, 1973). Women had entered the workforce in large numbers. Economic and educational opportunities for women widened, fertility rates had decreased. All this led to the growth of powerful women's movements in 1970s. Hence, Rosenberg concluded that court opinions were delivered into a political, economic and social system in which powerful forces were pushing for change. He held that "court decisions joined a current of social change and a tide of history; they did not create it".[19]

Though the court did not produce significant social reform, it eased access to safe and legal abortion and put the abortion issue on the public agenda. Luker has shown that although the Supreme Court decision had major effect on the practice of abortion, it did very little to change public attitudes.[20]

---

18. Blake, Judith, "The Abortion Decisions: Judicial Review and Public Opinion", in Manier, E., Liu, W., Soloman, D., (eds.), 1977 *Abortion New Direction for Policy Studies*, University of Notre Dame Press.
19. Rosenberg, Gerald N., 1991, *The Hollow Hope: Can Courts Bring About Social Change*, Chicago: The University of Chicago Press.
20. Luker, Kristin, 1984, *Abortion and the Politics of Motherhood*, USA: University of California Press.

In an interesting study William Mishler and R.S. Sheehan[21] have shown on the basis of Time Series Analysis for the period 1956-1989 that the court has been highly responsive to majority opinion. Its decisions not only have conformed closely to the aggregate policy opinions of the American public but have thereby reinforced and helped legitimate emergent majoritarian concerns.

Another argument usually advanced is that the Supreme Court justices are aware of the limitations of the court's power and its dependence on voluntary acquiescence to its decisions (Adamany and Grossman, 1983). As Justice Frankfurter expressed in the Baker v Carr case (1962): "The court's authority—possesed of neither the purse nor the sword—ultimately rests on sustained public confidence in its moral sanction."

The Supreme Court justice may be influenced by long-term changes in the climate of public opinion. For most of the period since 1956, a reciprocal relationship appears to have existed between the ideology of the public mood in the US and the broad ideological tenor of Supreme Court decisions. The court has been highly responsive to majority opinion. Its decisions not only have conformed closely to the aggregate policy opinion of the American public but have thereby reinforced and helped legitimate emergent of majoritarian concerns. However, since 1981, the relationship of the court and public opinion has turned different. The court's ideological balance has been upset by an unbroken string of conservative to moderate appointments, thereby changing the

21. Mischler, William and Sheehan, R.S., 1993, "The Supreme Court As a Counter Majoritarian Institution: The Impact of Public Opinion on Supreme Court", *American Political Science Review*, Vol.87, No.1, March.

ideological orientation of the court. The court grew increasingly conservative across this period despite a liberal resurgence in public mood.

Webster (1989) and Casey (1992) decisions shifted the venue of abortion policy from the federal judiciary to the state legislatures. However, empirical studies[22] show that majoritarian preferences of the mass public match up with state abortion policies. Impact of public opinion on abortion laws would become clearer if you examine the public attitudes which have influenced the opinion.

Public Attitudes and Public Opinion

Opinions are the result of complex values and belief calculations and actual life experiences.[23] Attitudes of American citizens toward abortion policy are rooted in conflicting core beliefs, value orientations, past experiences, and current life circumstances. Social, economic, demographic, religious and political variables influence a person's attitudes towards abortion and form the basis of group differences. Abortion approval varies to some extent by socio-demographic characteristics of the public, such as sex, race, age, education and income. Findings of most of the empirical studies reveal that religious variables are the most important in determining attitudes towards abortion (Arney and Trescher, 1976; Granberg and Granberg, 1981; Tedrow and Mahoney, 1979; Legge,

---

22. Wetstein, Mathew, E., 1996, *Abortion Rates in the U.S.: The Influence of Opinion and Policy*, Albany: State University of New York Press.

    Goggin, Malcolm, L., (ed.), 1993, *Understanding the New Politics of Abortion*, USA: Sage.
23. Bennett, L.W., 1980, *Public Opinion in American Politics*, USA: Harcourt Brace, Javanovich.

1983), while there have been denominational differences, Jews and mainstream Protestants being more supportive of abortion and Catholics and fundamentalists more opposed. The most striking finding is that most variation is limited to complex interaction between religion and church attendance. Attitudes on abortion are less a function of specific religious preference than they are of intensity of religious adherence.[24]

Regarding demographic variables, education has been the most consistent. Education appears to be the strongest predictor. An important part of the relationship between high levels of education and liberal attitudes towards legal abortion is clearly due to the socialising experiences of abortion. Citizens in high prestige job and who have high family incomes are also more supportive of legal abortion. Southerners and rural residents are less likely to support gender equality and are more likely to be conservative on questions of sexual morality and other issues. Abortion attitudes will differ across age groups. Different generations of citizens may hold different set of beliefs.[25] As a person's education increases, support for abortion rises. Race would also seem to an important variable, yet most empirical research on the subject demonstrates little difference between the races, with blacks being less supportive of abortion. This is despite the fact that actual utilisation of abortion by blacks is higher

---

24. Baker, Ross, K., Epstein, Laurily, K. and Forth, Rodney, D., 1981, "Matters of Life and Death: Social, Political and Religious Correlates of Attitudes on Abortion", *American Politics Quarterly*, Vol.9, No.1, January.

    Legge, Jerome, S. Jr., "Abortion as a Policy Issue: Attitudes of the Mass Public", *Women and Politics*, Vol. 7, No.1, Spring.
25. Cook, Elizabeth Adell, Jelen, Ted G. and Clyde, Wilcox, 1992, *Between Two Absolutes: Public Opinion and the Politics of Abortion*, USA: Westview Press.

than for the majority group. Cates (1977), and Combs and Welch (1982)[26] attribute this difference atleast partially to the greater religiosity of blacks. Age differences associated with abortion attitudes are not linear, and trend data show more conservative views among both very young and very old age groups (Ebaugh and Haney, 1978; Blake, 1984). The differences between sexes also appear to be slight. Until recently most survey research (Blake and del Pinal, 1980; Jacqueline Scott, 1989; Tedrow and Mahoney, 1979; Ebaugh and Haney, 1978) have shown that men tended to be slightly more liberal in their views than women, despite the fact that women suffer greater consequences in having an unwanted pregnancy. This could be due to the motherhood thesis which may be more important to women. Hence, women are more likely to feel that abortion is immorally wrong. But despite this moral reservation, women are more likely than men to favour legal abortion (Jacqueline Scott, 1989). With more education women are becoming more supportive than men. (Legge, 1983) Women of higher education and family income are more likely to approve of abortion. Urban and suburban residents are more likely to support legal abortion than those living in small towns or rural areas.

Finlay (1981) reports that men's attitudes vary primarily with their conventionality, whereas women's attitudes are more complex and are related to a broader set of attitudes, including the value they place on children, attitudes about the equality of men and women (Granberg, 1981; Luker, 1985) and ideological issues of abortion.

Ideological stance have become more important predictors of abortion attitudes than they were before the Supreme

---

26. Combs, M.W. and Welch, S., 1982, "Blacks, Whites, and Attitudes towards Abortion", *Public Opinion Quarterly*, 46: 510-20.

Court decision because of polarisation of abortion politics between pro-choice and pro-life platforms. Many empirical research have attempted to uncover the broader ideological structure underlying abortion attitudes (Barnatt and Harris, 1982; Blake, 1971; Blake and del Pinal, 1980; Falik, 1983; Deitch, 1983; Ebaugh and Haney, 1985; Findlay, 1985; Feldman, 1985; Granberg and Granberg, 1980, 1985; Scott and Schumann, 1988).

Attitudinal variables are more likely to influence the approval of abortion for social reasons (Barnatt and Harris, 1982). These will be helpful to understand the attitudes of the activists as well as the middle majority of the public. According to the findings of Sitaraman's empirical research (1994), public attitudes towards abortion centre around a balance among a respect for foetal life, an understanding of the pregnant woman's dilemma and a high emphasis a marital and family harmony in resolving reproductive decisions.

Pro-Choice v Pro-Life Debate

Abortion has been described as the "most controversial social issues of our time" (Scott and Schuman, 1988), a "conflict between core values" (Alverez and Brehm, 1995), a "clash between two absolutes" (Cook, Jelen and Wilcox, 1992; Tribe, 1992; Ginsberg, 1989). The status of abortion law has been subjected to judicial litigation. It has turned into a low intensity civil war, the battleground reaching from the Supreme Court to the Congress and the state legislatures, out to the pavements outside abortion clinics, where women have been systematically terrorised and doctors have been gunned down and killed.[27]

27. Hadley, Janet, 1996, *Abortion between Freedom and Necessity*.

Abortion policy remains a matter of intense debate, where there are two identifiable groups of activists: anti-abortion ("pro-life") groups that advocate restrictive policies; and pro-abortion ("pro-choice") groups that advocate a permissive policy allowing a woman to choose.

Advocates of pro-choice, inspired by secular humanism, believe that abortion is a basic human right.[28] They attach moral value to the woman's right to her own body against state or social interference. They assert that the women must be free to decide whether to continue or discontinue her pregnancy. They do not recognise the unborn as a person. The rights of the woman supercede those of the foetus. Abortion rights advocates maintain that law should leave decision making in this area to the individual citizens most concerned. Permissive laws enhance the freedom of those who believe that they should be able to elect abortion in accordance with conscience.

For the pro-life movement, on the other hand, abortion is equivalent to murder. They believe that human life begins at conception and the right to life override all other rights and interests. They are committed to the re-establishment of the rights of the foetus as a person. They seek an America in which every unborn child is protected in law and welcomed in life. Their contention is strongly supported by fundamentalist Protestants, Orthodox Jews, and the Catholic Church. Right to life advocates perceive any move toward liberalisation as an assault on traditional family values and gender roles. To them abortion undermines marriage, morality and motherhood. A statement of pro-life principle and concern categorically holds that a sweeping abortion license was granted by the Supreme Court which has wounded the

28. Steinem, G., 1989, "A Basic Human Right", MS, July/April.

American democracy, has eroded the moral foundations of the American civic community, led to national virtue deficit, kills 1.5 million innocent human beings in America every year, hurts women by encouraging widespread male irresponsibility and has contributed to the marginalisation of fatherhood in America. They felt that the abortion license threatened the cultural foundations of their democratic political community. It was unilaterally defined by the Supreme Court without recourse to democratic debate and legislation.[29]

The abortion issue arouses a level of intensity among activists that is seldom seen in American politics. Two cleavages underlie the antagonism between these contending forces. One, sectarian, reflects deep theological differences in how Jews, Protestants, and Catholics view the act of creation. But more significant is the secular battle over the status of women and the child bearing role within the traditional family and the larger society. The root cause of the abortion conflict is a clash of moral ideals (Tatalovich and Daynes, 1993). Research shows that those inclined to the pro-life position are generally influenced by a conservative traditional and sacred ideology (Falik, 1983). They are guided by a familial orientation. They tend to favour large families (Granbergs, 1978, 1981, 1982) and believe that women's primary role is to produce and nourish life (Luker, 1984). For them abortion is a moral issue (Smetana, 1982). The foetus is a life at conception, and taking away that life is immoral.

Those inclined towards pro-choice are generally influenced by a liberal, modern, secular ideology (Falik, 1983). They tend to be advocates of individual rights, in particular,

29. "The America We Seek: A Statement of Prolife Principle and Concern", *National Review*, March 25, 1996.

women's right to have control over reproduction. While having a family may be satisfying, motherhood is not the only role for women (Luker, 1984). For pro-choice, abortion is a personal issue (Smetna, 1982). The foetus is an independent life at birth. Aborting the foetus gives women choices they would otherwise not have. Scott, in her study (1989), documents that opponents of abortion are much more absolute and rule bound in their moral stance than are those who support legal abortion. Those who are pro-life tend to have more unified attitude structures, while those who are pro-choice tend to have less unified attitude structures (Stets and Leik, 1993).

Judicial decisions generated a vigorous organised opposition that sought legislative and constitutional amendment restricting access to abortion. The right to life movement resulted in the passage of the Hyde amendment banning federal funding for abortion in 1976. In 1989 in the Webster v Reproductive Health Services case, the US Supreme Court granted states more freedom to place additional restrictions on abortions by prohibiting federal medicaid funding for abortion. Webster however acted as a catalyst for the pro-choice group to mobilise its supporters. Again, the Supreme Court's decision in Planned Parenthood of Southeastern Pennyslvains v Casey reaffirmed its increasing tolerance of restrictive abortion statutes of the states.

Abortion politics in the US reveals an unusually large impact of a committed and passionate minority. Why is it that the opponents of abortion are becoming more effective politically at a time when public support and acceptance of abortion seems to be increasing. Luker (1984) gave three reasons for this: intensity of their commitment; secondly, use of new communication techniques to translate that commitment into new political resources; and thirdly, willingness of pro-life supporters to make their position on abortion the role determinant of their political behaviour.[30] Thus, the pro-life movement has been politically successful despite growing public support for abortion, in part because it has been intensely committed to the goal of outlawing abortion during a period when the general public has been only weakly committed to supporting it. Mansbridge similarly stated that "the attempt to ban legal abortion has remained a live issue only because its advocates feel so passionately about it, while many opponents are ambivalent."[31] Pro-life groups enjoyed considerable success at the state level in restricting Medicaid funded abortions. Pro-life supporters were successful because of intensity of their commitment and involvement and their single issue focus. Scott's (1989) study documents that moral beliefs of the opponents of abortion reinforce their legal stance whereas the moral dilemma of the pro-choice supporters undermines their willingness to promote their cause.[32]

The universe of abortion rights opinion seem to be made up of three groups: those who are absolutely against abortion, except perhaps to save the woman's life; those who favour abortion on demand; and those whose position depends on the circumstances.[33] Majority of the public support legal abortion in some, but not all circumstances (Grangberg and Grangberg, 1980; Lamenna, 1984). They favour some restrictions on abortion but do not support an absolute ban. Clyde Wilcox has called this middle category 'situationalists'

---

30. Luker, K., supra note 20.
31. Mansbridge, Jane, 1986, *Why We Lost the ERA*, Chicago: University of Chicago Press.
32. Scott, J., 1989, "Conflicting beliefs about abortion: Legal approval and moral doubt", *Social Psychological Quarterly*, 52:319-26.
33. Craig, B.H. and O'Brian, D.M., supra note 13.

who support legal abortion in some situations but not in others.[34]

Majority of the people demonstrate considerable ambivalence of attitudes (Blake and del Pinal, 1981; Siber, 1980). Alice S. Rossi and Sitaram's study (1988) highlights the significant fact that majority of the people do not hold strong views about abortion, most are fence sitters who feel considerable ambivalence toward legal abortion.

More Americans support abortion for 'hard' reasons, circumstances that involve physical trauma, but deeply divided over circumstances that are more social in origin.

On the hard reasons of abortion the public is closer to the pro-choice while on the soft or discretionary reasons for abortion the public may be slightly closer to the pro-life position. A significant fraction remains ambivalent, wanting to keep access to abortion legal, but regulating the access. Everett Carll Ladd[35] has documented that majority feel that abortion should not be categorically banned but it should not be established as an absolute right. Policy should seek a balance between the mother's claim to choose and the claim accruing to all human life.

Thus, public sentiments toward abortion are often based on conflicting values. This decreases the strength with which abortion attitudes are held and in turn diminishes the potential of these attitudes to translate into politically relevant behaviour. The partial victory of the pro-life movement to

---

34. Wilcox, Clyde,1992, "Race, Region, Religion and Abortion Attitudes: Some Additional Evidence", *Public Opinion, Quarterly*, 54:284-55.
35. Ladd, E.C., 1989, "The Partisan Consequences", *Public Opinion*, American Enterprise Institute, May-June.

change Roe v Wade standards illustrate the success of an intense minority. The success of pro-choice groups will depend upon the ability to mobilise those members of the public who hold ambivalent attitudes on the issue.[36] Inglehart[37] (1990) suggests that the process of generational replacement will result in more liberal mass publics in the western nations. The younger cohorts are more liberal on feminist issues than older ones. The 1990s saw the increasing politicisation of the abortion issue, with the National Republican Party officially adopting an anti-abortion position and most National Democrats publicly endorsing legal abortion. Although Webster and Casey constituted a backlash to the struggle for the pro-choice movement. However, the pro-choice position still attracts more supporters than the idea of outlawing abortion under all circumstances.

Impact of Public Attitudes on Abortion

Only if public opinion is unambiguous and clear it can have a significant impact over public policy. When public opinion regarding abortion is ambiguous, symbolic restrictions with little policy impact may result.[38] Policy making is responsive to both public opinion and interest group activity.

Due to the ambiguity of the majority, pro-life movement

---

36. Goggin, M.L., 1993, "Understanding the New Politics of Abortion: A Framework and Agenda for Research", *American Politics Quarterly*, 21:4-30.
37. Inglehart, R., 1990, *Culture Shift in Advanced Industrial Society*, Princeton New Jersey: Princeton University Press.
38. Hansen, Susan, B., 1990, "State Differences in Public Policies Towards Women: A Test of Three Hypotheses", paper presented at the annual meeting of the American Political Science Association, San Francisco.

succeeded in effecting state laws. Wavering and uncertain attitudes of the people may be less important than the well planned strategy and commitment of key members in effecting change. Rossi and Sitaraman's findings are that abortion as an issue is not considered a top priority by voters. It is not a partisan issue. Since majority of the people fall in the middle category, such a situation contributes to the confusion in investigating abortion as a cue to voting behaviour.[39]

Though Democratic and Republican leaders are, as groups, far apart on abortion, rank and file members of the two parties, however, for the most part hold strikingly similar views on the issue.[40]

As abortion poses a moral dilemma, remains a controversial and emotional issue, its implementation has not been easy. A central factor in the development of abortion policy in the US since 1973 is the failure of key actors in both the health care system and government to exercise leadership in the implementation of abortion policy. This is particularly so with the medical profession, the hospital leadership and the federal government. The system failed to respond in ways commensurate with its social role and responsibility.[41]

America's pro-life groups found ways to influence court decisions, politicians and legislatures in imposing restrictions on access to abortion services at state level. It is the issue of government funding of abortions that divides the states populations so powerfully. Given the confused and divided

39. Smith, T.W., 1996, GSS Project Report No.20, National Opinion Research Centre, Chicago: University of Chicago.
40. Ladd, E.C., supra note 25.
41. Lee, P.R. and LeRoy, L.B., "Abortion Politics and Public Policy", in Sachdev, P., (ed.), 1985, *Perspectives on Abortion*, New Jersey: Sacrecrow Press.

state of public opinion and an organised and vocal minority rejecting government support of abortion rights programmes, there is little reason to think that a coherent and consistent abortion rights policy has any chances of implementation. An equally coherent abortion policy would imply right of any woman to obtain an abortion implemented by programmes and practices and public funds that ensured that any woman who wanted an abortion could get one.[42]

Public opinion about abortion, despite all its inconsistencies and confusing contradictions, will play a far more important role in structuring public policy on the issue in the future.[43]

The debate over abortion has been monopolised by two extreme positions—that abortion is an unconditional human right, and it is invariably a crime. The American public is not entirely comfortable with either position. They disapprove of abortion that seem casual and capricious but are generally supportive of legal abortion in cases where the mother's health is in danger, in cases of rape or incest, or when there is a strong visibility of foetal defect.

Although public opinion on abortion is complex, it has been remarkably clear and consistent over the past decades. At the national level, public opinion changed for the first time in favour of legal abortion in the period 1966-1972. The Supreme Court decision in 1973 simply reflects this change in public opinion. Blake (1972 and 1980), Tatalovich (1982), Granbergs (1980) and Luker (1984) support this con-

---

42. Callahan, Daniel, 1979, "Abortion and Government Policy", *Family Planning Perspectives*, Vol.II, No.5, September-October.

43. Craig, Barkara, Hinkson and O'Brien, David M., 1993, *Abortion and American Politics*, Chatham, New Jersey: Chatham House Publishers, Inc.

tention that public opinion led the court. The court's decision was simply a consequence of the change in public opinion at the national level. The court's impact was primarily to increase the polarisation of groups on the issue with little or no increase in overall approval.[44] Similarly, the anti-abortion Webster case followed a wild conservative drift in opinion and indications in 1982 and 1984, that abortion opponents held their views more strongly than supporters (Scott and Schumann, 1988). In fact, the effects of Roe (1973) and Webster (1989) upon public opinion were largely neutralised by each decision's mobilisation of its opponents (Page and Shapiro, 1992).

On the other hand, in the US, public policy varied depending on the variations in state level public opinion. Empirical research (Wright, Erikson and MacIver, 1987) shows that state policies follow the ideological dispositions of the people who live there. Goggin and Kim's study (1992) indicates that state abortion policy does follow state public preferences, although the effect of abortion opinion is mediated by the preferences of the state political factors that make abortion policy, namely governors and legislators. Goggin and Kim's findings are consistent with the considerable literature that generally corroborates a linkage between public preferences and public policy (e.g., Weissberg, 1976; Monroe, 1979; Page and Shaprio, 1983, 1992; Wright, Erikson and MacIver, 1987).

Generally, opinions over a long period remain stable. Majority reject what they take to be the extremism of both the pro-life and pro-choice position in favour of what they characterise as a moderate's position. There is a public space between the absolutes of the "right to life" and the "right to

44. Franklin, C.H. and Kosaki, L.C., supra note 17.

choose".[45] Future debate on abortion should be conducted within this space. Faye D. Ginsberg in *Contested Lives* (1989)[46] and Lawrence H. Tribe in *Abortion: The Clash of Absolutes* (1993)[47] seek to find common ground between the claims of the two extreme positions. They favour strategies of rapprochement and hope that women could limit in a common struggle, and work for a social policy that would create a society of caring and responsible people. Ginsberg feels that the opposing sides have a common interest in helping women with unplanned pregnancies. Tribe argued that debate's current focus on 'absolutes', women's right to liberty and foetus right to life is over simplified and counter productive, and suggested that both sides work towards a world of only wanted pregnancies.

Abortion represents a case of public opinion clashing with interest groups. Pro-choice sentiment is more common among the mass public than is the pro-life sentiment. Yet, a significant fraction of the populace is somewhat ambivalent, wanting to keep access to abortion legal, but regulating the access. When opinion is narrowly decided, interest groups in opposition may prevail. And, even when opinion is at landside proportions, interest groups may still win about half of the time. Only when opinion is nearly consensual will public opinion consistently defeat organised interests. Policy making is responsive to both public opinion and interest groups. Only when the public speaks uniformly and consensually in support of a policy direction, can the system be mobilised

45. Jelen, Ted G. and Wilcox, C., supra note 5.
46. Ginsberg, Faye D., 1989, *Contested Lives: The Abortion Debate in an American Community*, Berkeley: University of California Press.
47. Tribe, L.H., 1992, *Abortion and the Clash of Absolutes*, New York: W.W. Norton & Co.

easily and swiftly to accord with public preference.[48]

Sometimes elites and interest groups may try to mould specific issues and contain the influence of public opinion. Impact of public opinion on public policy may be restricted in case of strong interest group activity. For example, in case of abortion, public opinion became generally supportive of making abortion legal, especially in certain traumatic situations. But pro-life activists restricted women's access to legal abortion.

Politics of abortion has been shaped by the courts and driven by interest group activists. Public opinion has influenced the making of public policy and will continue to play a significant role.

48. Cohen, Jeffrey, E. and Barrilleaux, Charles, "Public Opinion, Interest Groups and Public Policy Making, Abortion Policy in American States", in Goggin, M.L., (eds.), 1993, *Understanding The New Politics of Abortion*, New Delhi: Sage.

Appendix I

Percentage of US Adults Approving of Legal Abortion in Various Circumstances, * *Various Years, (1965-1980)*
("Abortion Attitudes, 1965-1980: Trends and Determinants", by Donald Granberg and Beth Wellman Granberg)

Circumstance	*1965*	*1972*	*1973*	*1974*	*1975*	*1976*	*1977*	*1978*	*1980*
"Please tell me whether you think it should be possible for a pregnant woman to obtain a legal abortion:									
(1) If the woman"s health is seriously endangered by the pregnancy	73	87	92	92	91	91	90	91	90
(2) If she became pregnant as a result of rape	59	79	83	86	84	84	84	83	83
(3) If there is a strong chance of a serious defect in the baby	57	79	84	85	83	84	85	82	83
(4) If the family has a very low income and cannot afford any more children	22	49	53	55	53	53	53	47	52
(5) If she is not married and does not want to marry the man	18	43	49	50	48	50	50	41	48
(6) If she is married and does not want any more children	16	40	48	47	46	46	46	40	47
For any reason"	na	na	na	na	na	na	38	33	41
Average approval for the six secified reasons	41	63	68	69	67	68	68	64	67

* All percentage are based on the number of those answering yes or no. Respondents who said they did not know or who did not give a yes-or-no answer were excluded from the analysis.
In this and subsequent tables, na=question not asked in that year.

Source: Family Planning Perspectives, Vol. 12, No.5, September/October 1980.

IV

Dowry in India: Origin and Present Status

Dowry is deeply rooted in the socio-cultural system of India. It has been so intimately linked with the custom that it has become legitimised in the subconscious minds of the people and is not regarded as immoral and illegal.

Modern dowry is different from the ancient custom of '*varadakshina*' or gift as prevalent among the upper castes and the '*sulka*' or brideprice as existing amongst the lower castes. Somewhere, in the process of civilisation, the two different practices adopted by the rich and the poor seem to have got incorporated and what emerged finally is what we see in the form of dowry today.[1]

In the old 'Brahma' form of marriage which was peculiar to the upper castes, '*kanyadan*', the gift of the daughter to the

1. Butalia, Subhadra, 1983, "Dowry and Attitudes", *Women's Link*, Newsletter, No.18, March.

learned groom, accompanied with presents in cash or kind known as '*varadakshina*'. Both these were considered meritorious acts and not as a sale of a son. It was essentially a gift pure and simple. The presents and jewellery were voluntarily given out of pure affection and presented no impediment in the settlement of daughter's marriage.

In 'Asura' form of marriage, prevalent amongst the poor sections, the custom was just the reverse as they practised 'brideprice'. The husband used to get a bride by paying a reasonable price called '*sulka*' to her parents or guardian. This practice was condemned by the *Smriti* writers. Since brideprice was deemed equivalent to the sale of a daughter, it was judged reprehensible. In its place, Manu commends the gift of the virgin daughter in the *kanyadan* ceremony. Gradually, the poorer sections began emulating the upper castes as a result of sanskritisation.[2]

Gradually, dowry which in the ancient times was more or less a voluntary practice, assumed commercial overtones. In the medieval time pre-puberty marriages came into vogue and dowry became the dominant factor in settlement of marriage. It became a positive evil of great magnitude in Rajputana from the 13th century.[3] At first practised by the upper castes, it slowly percolated down to the lower castes and classes and by the middle of the 19th century it assumed alarming proportions. In the contemporary Hindu society, dowry has become a commercial transaction. Today the groom's party often demands a complete inventory of ornaments, cash etc., that will accompany the bride, before the

---

2. Achar, M.R. and Vekannas, T., 1986, *Dowry Prohibition Act and Rules*, Allahabad: The Law Book Co.
3. Kumari, Ranjana, 1989, *Brides Are Not For Burning*, New Delhi: Radiant Publisher.

marriage proposal is accepted.

The modern practice of dowry has no semblance to the original concept contained in the Hindu law as it originated in the ancient times. Paras Diwan is very categorical that the present system of dowry does not have its origin in '*kanyadan*' or '*varadakshina*'. For '*varadakshina*' prevailed only among certain castes of Brahmins. For '*varadakshina*' was voluntary while dowry is demanded. Further, dowry should not be confused with '*stridhan*'. Latter is the property in the form of cash, ornaments, clothes and other articles willingly gifted to a daughter at or about or subsequently to marriage. The donee (daughter) has absolute right to dispose of such property as she likes. As '*stridhan*' was considered to be the absolute property of a Hindu married woman, it gave her a kind of financial security under adverse circumstances. Dowry is most derogatory to the dignity of women. It is seldom in control of the girl, for it is immediately appropriated by the husband's family. Dowry, according to Diwan, has always been, conceptually and essentially, that property which is obtained under duress, coercion or pressure, is extorted, extracted or even snatched away from the parents or guardians of the girl by the bridegroom or his parents or other near relations.[4]

The present-day dowry has neither anything traditional about it nor is it sanctioned by Hindu religion. It has reduced marriage into a commercial transaction and assumed compulsive character. The observation of the report of the Joint Parliamentary Committee appointed to examine the Dowry Prohibition Act, 1961 is very significant. It held that dowry is

4. Diwan, Paras, 1997, *Law Relating to Dowry, Dowry Deaths, Bride Burning, Rape and Related Offence*, New Delhi: Universal Law Pub Co.

not one isolated payment initially at the time of marriage but a series of gifts given over a period of time before and after marriage. Compulsion, coercion and even violence are now being used to obtain dowry, thus making most Hindu marriages, a bargain. Dowry has assumed menacing proportions, and has spread to all castes and classes and communities in Indian society.

Modern dowry, as M.N. Srinivas holds, is entirely the product of the forces let loose by British rule such as monetisation, education, and the introduction of the 'organised' sector.[5] The National Committee on the Status of Women in India[6] has pointed to the increasing withdrawal of women from the labour force and productive activities. This has made the girl in her father's family a liability rather than an asset. Dowry replaced '*stridhan*' and 'brideprice' as a compensation for the lower economic value of women not working or employed. Dowry reflects more dependent relations of women in production and in the control of resources.[7] Within this context, dowry demands that are the catalysts of dowry deaths, are one of a number of attempts for men to raise their status, at the expense of women. Thus, dowry is the manifestation of the political, economic and cultural insignificance of women, both in her natal family and in the family in which she enters after marriage.[8] Dowry is the

---

5. Srinivas, M.N., 1983, *Some Reflections and Dowry*, Bombay: Oxford University Press.
6. *Towards Equality: Report of the Committee on the Status of Women in India*, New Delhi: Government of India, 1974
7. McCoid, Catherine, Hodge, 1989, "Dowry Deaths in India: A Materialistic Analysis", Central Missouri State University, Working Paper.
8. Jethmalani, Rani, Dey, P.K., "Dowry Deaths and Access to Justice", in Jethmalani, Rani, (ed.), 1995, *Kali's Yug, Empowerment Law and Dowry*, WARLAW, New Delhi: Haranand.

symbol of women's oppression. It perpetuates her inferior status in her matrimonial home and has led to harassments and dowry deaths.

Dowry is based on the cultural ethos which views brides as objects to be passed from one social group to another. The declining status of women in modern India is visible in the adverse sex ratio which reflected male child preference, lower life expectancy of females, early marriage of girls, high female mortality, earlier in the form of female infanticide, now foeticide, unequal access to health care, inadequate nutritional intake. The practice of dowry has often been seen as a major factor in this development.

Social Scientists have Interpreted Dowry in Different Ways

Dowry as a Gift

The most common interpretation of dowry is as a gift from the brides family to the groom at the time of her wedding. Gift giving constitutes social links between the partners of the exchange. In the Hindu tradition, '*kanyadan*', the gift of the bride, must be accompanied by token gift called '*varadakshina*'. According to the scriptures, gift giving bestowed a status on the giver and implied a reciprocity. But dowry in modern India accords inferior status to the giver. Present form of dowry often involving large amounts of cash is demanded even after the marriage, whereas the traditional form was a one time gift at the time of marriage.[9] Dowry is a recurring phenomena, a bargain made before marriage with constant demands at every festival or whenever there is

9. Paul, Madan, 1985, *Dowry and Position of Women in India: A Study of Delhi Metropolis*, New Delhi: Inter India.

monetary need.[10] Hence, dowry has coercive overtones and cannot be equated to gift which is given voluntarily.

Dowry as Premortem Inheritance

Dowry is sometimes seen as female property or female right to property which is transferred at her marriage as a sort of premortem inheritance. Goody[11] regards dowry as a mode of "diverging devolution" in which daughters receive their share which, upon her marriage, joins her husband's assets to form a conjugal fund. According to Tambiah,[12] dowry in India reflects female right to (movable not patrimonial) property as ensured in the concept of '*stridhanam*'. According to the Hindu scriptures '*stridhan*' belongs exclusively to the woman and was given voluntarily, while modern dowry is compulsorily extracted in consideration of marriage. T.N. Madan argues that dowry can be seen as a 'substitute' for women's lack of rights of inheritance, rather than as a form of inheritance rights. In fact, he preferred to regard dowry as a compensation for daughter's lack of inheritance equivalent to those of men. Dowry, as Bina Agarwal points out, cannot be demanded as a right as is the case with inheritance (*Indian Express*, July 9, 1989). Several studies have shown that women do not have any control over the items they take with them as dowry to their husband's family (Madan, 1965;

10. Chhabra, Sagari, 1986, *Dowry Death in India: A Double Bind Perspective* (A Thesis for M.A. in Communication), Washington State University, Department of Communications.
11. Goody, Jack, "Bridewealth and Dowry in Africa and Eurasia", in Goody, Jack and Tambiah, S.J., (eds.), 1973, *Bridewealth and Dowry*, Cambridge: Cambridge University Press.
12. Tambiah, S.J., "Dowry Bridewealth and Property Rights", in Goody, J. and Tambiah, S.J., (eds.), 1973, *Bridewealth and Dowry*, Cambridge: Cambridge University Press.

Srinivas, 1984; Kumari, 1989). In fact, with the enactment of the Hindu Succession Act, 1956, it was hoped that dowry would vanish when women would receive equal inheritance right. However, inferior position of women's inheritance rights continued and the custom of dowry persisted in all its ugliness. Dowry is chiefly due to women's extremely subservient status in marriage and family. Dowry cannot be equated with inheritance, holds Madhu Kishwar. For woman has no control over her dowry, it is not equal to the share of a son, the goods given in dowry are not income generating forms of property, unlike the property normally given to a son.

Dowry as Compensation

Dowry is also seen as compensation to the man's family for the allegedly economically unproductive woman. In modern India, dowry is more common in northern India, where woman's participation in labour force in low (Bardhan, 1982; Miller, 1981; Rajaraman, 1983). This view is too economically deterministic. It ignores the value of the domestic work done by women and growing participation of women in economic activity and significance of social and cultural factors. Women are economically not unproductive. She performs the important family labour which is never taken into account.

Dowry Related to Hypergamy

Blunt (1969) attributes dowry to hypergamy. Hindus had a tendency towards hypergamy, whereby a family of lower status but not necessarily of inferior wealth, attempted to raise its position and prestige by contracting a superior marriage for its daughters. Here there was an exchange of status for wealth in form of dowry. The girl's family purchases the upward social mobility through dowry. However, this view ignores the asymmetrical gender relations in the society and merely focuses on the caste structure. For higher dowries now go to grooms with a higher earning capacity even if they be of lower social status. Moreover, in placing the emphasis on hypergamy practised by the woman's family, the role of dowry in negotiating status for the man's family in the context of the growing significance of class over caste in India, remains unexplored.[13] The social status markers are now different, this however does not affect the earlier significance of hypergamy.

'Brideprice' has been replaced by 'groomprice' system, characterised by the transfer of large sums of cash, jewellery and other goods from the bride's family to the groom's family. This can be seen as an outcome of the growth of the capitalist economy and the consequent emergence of a class system based on wealth. Jamila Verghese's study has revealed the price attached to different categories of grooms like teachers, lecturers, engineers, doctors, IFS and IAS officers etc. She has traced the deterioration from being gifts of affection to becoming a means of extortion and exploitation.[14] Dowry, according to M.C. Paul[15], serves three purposes:

(i) A means of directly compensating the daughter for her lack of rights of inheritance.

(ii) Parents concern to provide the daughter financial security and elevate her status in the conjugal household.

(iii) Public demonstration of the means and standing of the

13. Chauhan, Richa, 1995, *Dowry in the Twentieth Century India: A Window to Conflict of Caste, Class, and Gender* (A Dissertation in Sociology), Stony Brook: State University of New York.
14. Vergese, Jamila, 1980, *Her Body, Her Gold*, New Delhi: Vikas.
15. Paul, M.C., supra note 9.

natal family. Dowry has taken the shape of status symbol both for the donor, and recipient families. Paul's study reveals that dowry was increasingly practised in urban Delhi, amongst the new rich and educated sections.

S.L. Hooja[16] holds that the dowry system arose mainly out of regard for the daughter, respect for the family and fulfilment of religion. It has grown into a rigid custom of great social evil and has become associated with social and family prestige.

Dowry in modern India has been particularly shaped by two factors: the inferior social status of the wife's family, relative to that of the husband, and the exclusion of women from the inheritance of immovable property.[17] From the perspective of the bride's family, dowry payments involve trading present consumption for the future earning power of their daughter through acquiring a groom with high earning potential.[18]

With the urbanisation and consumerism characterising India today, women are valued for the dowry they will bring. So long as their valuation rests primarily in their being vehicles of property transmission, they will remain vulnerable to dowry harassment and murder.[19]

---

16. Hooja, S.L., 1969, *Dowry System in India: A Case Study*, New Delhi: Asia Press.
17. Stein, Dorothy, 1988, "Burning Widows, Burning Brides The Perils of Daughterhood in India", *Pacific Affairs*, Vol.61, No.3.
18. Willigen, J.V. and Channa, V.C., 1991, "Law, Custom and Crimes Against Women: The Problem of Dowry Death in India", *Human Organisation*, Vol.50, No.4.
19. Stone, Lind, James, Caroline, 1995, "Dowry Bride Burning, and Femalẹ Power in India", *Women's Studies International Forum*, Vol.15, No.2.

Richa Chauhan's study[20] has revealed certain interesting facts. Modernisation and industrialisation led to fading of dowry prevalent in England, Germany, France, Italy and Brazil. But, in India, it has led to escalation in dowry demands. Dowry has reshaped itself to conform to a more contemporary market-based industrial and urban Indian society. Dowry is no longer confined to the upper castes among the Hindus, it has spread to lower castes as well as non-Hindu communities such as Muslims and Christians in India. Consumer items and large amounts of cash are openly demanded by the groom's family. Dowry has become increasingly contractual, often leading to violence against women. Caste, class and '*pativrata*' ideology are the key factors for explaining the change and persistence of dowry in India. The first or the gift phase (1900-1947) corresponds to the pre-independence India and ends in 1947, when dowry was modest and voluntary and retained its gift form. The second phase (1948-1961), the contractual phase, corresponds to post-independence India and culminates in 1961, the year when Dowry Prohibition Act made dowry illegal. In the second phase, with industrialisation and modernisation and growth of consumerism, dowry demands became blatant and open often leading to harassment and violence. The final phase, the abusive phase, where dowry became increasingly coercive, and its emergence as a major cause of domestic abuse especially after 1920. This was due to dislocation between caste and class and increased isolation of women because of the extremely patriarchal structure of the marriage and dependent position of women in the family. However, Chauhan asserts that there were no clear-cut transformation as in the form of dowry, but

20. Chauhan, R., supra note 13.

rather present a continuum of change in the form of dowry.

Dowry in the gift phase was modest and voluntary, confined to the upper castes, but sanskritisation led to the adoption of the practice of dowry in the lower castes. As a result Dowry Prohibition Act was passed in 1961 to combat the growing menace. Moreover, in contemporary India, along with caste, importance of income, education and occupation of the group are considered in arranged marriages. This has resulted in the contractual nature of dowry and spread of dowry to non-Hindu communities and even in southern parts of India. Insufficient dowry usually took the form of physical abuse or desertion by the husband, often ending in murder or suicides, known as dowry deaths. Chauhan's study asserts that abuse due to dowry comes from inferior status of women.

Dowry has become inseparably interlinked with the status of women in our society. It has massive social sanctions behind it and cannot be curbed by progressive laws.[21] The Hindu woman does not have an independent identity, her identity is wholly defined by her relationship to others. An ancient law, as given by Manu says: "In childhood a female must be subject to her father, in youth her husband, when her lord is dead to her sons. A woman must never be independent."[22] Thus, she is first a daughter, next a wife and a the mother, never an independent person in her own right.

A daughter is normally an unmitigated expense, someone who will never contribute to the family income and who upon marriage will take away a considerable part of her family's fortune as her dowry. This cultural devaluation of

21. Kumari, Ranjana, supra note 13.
22. Manu, V., 148.

women has heightened their feelings of worthlessness and inferiority.[23]

The Hindu woman is socialised to believe that marriage is her destiny, her only hope of salvation. From the beginning, the girl child is taught that her only aim in life is to get married and be a dutiful wife. "Though destitute of virtue, a husband must be constantly worshipped as a God by a faithfull wife", holds Manu[24] The Hindu notion of the ideal woman is the woman who is completely devoted to her husband, living or dead.

Such virtuous wife is described as '*pativrata*' which implies unquestioned devotion to husband, in fact no existence apart from that of her husband. Such an ideology leads to the development of a personality characterised by compliance, docility and low self-esteem. The ideal woman is one who looks down upon herself and lives for others.[25]

Indian women are adopting the modernised version of '*pativrata*' by combining the role of an educated or employed women with that of a dutiful wife, sacrificing mother and an obedient daughter-in-law.[26] Motherhood and the ideal of a faithful, loyal, self-sacrificing wife continue to be projected through the media and the education system. Her total dependence and "marriage at all cost" syndrome forces her to put up with harassment and violence within marriage. The Indian society, according to Meera Kosambi, remains firmly rooted in the patriarchal ideology which is premised upon male supremacy and a legitimisation of women's oppression.

---

23. Chhabra, R., supra note 10.
24. Manu V., 154.
25. Dhruvrajan, Vanaja, 1981, *Hindu Women and Power of Ideology*, Massachusetts: Bergin and Harvey Pub. Inc.
26. Chauhan, R., supra note 13.

It treats her primarily as an instrument of male sexual enjoyment and of reproduction of children. Marriage being central to Hindu woman's life. Through marriage a man acquires property right over his wife.[27]

Similarly, Govind Kelkar relates violence against women to aspects of structural violence and forms of control and coercion exercised through an hierarchical and patriarchal gender relationship in the family and society. Dowry is rooted in women's subordination in the structure of material production. Men tend to value their roles as breadwinners and supporters of the family while women are excessively undervalued because of their dependence, ignorance and preoccupation with household chores. Only if a fundamental change is made in the existing propertylessness and resourcelessness of women, would women have inalienable rights to land, property and inheritance. The existing unequal wage system should be rectified, only then can violence against women be combatted.[28]

Dowry, the symbol of women's oppression, has perpetuated her inferior status, devalued her, made her a liability to be disposed off at a discount in the inter-family transaction, that is marriage. In its present form, it operates as part of a system that disinherits the daughter not just materially but morally. It increases her dependency and symbolises the un-

27. Kosambi, Meera, (ed.), 1994, *Women's Oppression in the Public Gaze*, Bombay: SNDT,Women's University.

—, "Tradition, Modernity and Violence Against Women", in Shirin, Kudchedkar, Sabi, (ed.), 1995, *Violence Against Women*, New Delhi: A1-Pencraft International.

28. Kelkar, Govind, 1985, "Women and Structural Violence in India", Occasional Paper, No.4, New Delhi: CWDS.

—, 1992, *Violence Against Women: Perspectives and Strategies in India*, Shimla:IIAS.

equal power relation between the man and woman. The most important change would be the delinking of property ownership from marriage and ensuring that parents do not disinherit their daughters.[29] Men have been generally opposed to equal inheritance rights for women on the ground that it would create discord between brothers and sisters. Hooja (1969) had earlier pointed out that if we replace dowry by property rights, men will seek to marry the woman with the largest properly. Hooja refers to dowry as "unspiritual in nature" with no ethical value.

Hindu laws of property and ownership of the means of production give women negligible rights as independent entities to family income, assets and property. In most cases, daughters wave their rights in favour of their brothers. The economic dependency on man for survival keeps woman a passive prisoner. A woman's economic dependency compel her to remain in the matrimonial home. Madhu Kishwar holds that unless such a time as the law of inheritance are transformed enabling women to claim their rightful entitlement to property, women should not be deprived of their dowries.[30] This viewpoint has been opposed by most of the activists.

However, Bina Agarwal holds that realising inheritance rights for women is crucial, but women should not accept dowry as a substitute, even in the interim. For dowry is not

---

29. Kishwar, Madhu, 1989, "Towards More Just Norms of Marriage: Continuing the Dowry Debate", *Manushi*, No.58.
    —, 1986, "To Ensure Her Happiness or To Disinherit Her?", *Manushi*, No.34.
30. Kishwar, M., 1988, "Rethinking Dowry Boycott", *Manushi*, No. 48.
    —, 1989, "Dowry and Inheritance Rights", *EPW*, Vol. XXIV, No. 11, March 18.

the most effective way of increasing women's bargaining power and cannot substitute for effective rights in inheritance. Parents who have once given a daughter dowry will be unlikely to concede her demand for inheritance as well. It is essential to abolish the advantages that males in several states enjoy under the Hindu Succession Act of 1956, due to the retention of the Mitakshara coparcenary system which gives sons certain property rights that daughters do not have. It is also necessary to restrict the power of testation under the 1956 Act to safeguard the interests of daughters who may otherwise be disinherited by parents through wills. It is essential to establish women's de facto inheritance right in land. Unless females are allowed to exercise control over their property rights, until they actually control their earned money, the problem of dowry will persist, because dowry is rooted in unequal economic relations between man and woman. Women alone can take a stand.[31] Dowry is sustained both by women's economic dependency within the family and the dominant familial ideology that sustains this dependency. Equal inheritance rights and equal remuneration should be stressed. Women should be given coparcenary right to property. The daughter should not be allowed to sign away her property rights in favour of male relatives. No such transactions should be considered valid.

Uprooting Dowry Through Law

The Indian Constitution tried to promote equal rights through the instrument of law. Despite wide ranging protective legislations, women continue to face a great deal of discrimination in public and private life. The Committee on

31. Agrawal, Bina, 1994, *A Field of One's Own: Gender and Land Rights in South Asia*, New Delhi: Cambridge University Press.

the Status of Women in India (1974), in its report, held that women are not conscious partners in the social processes of change. They are unequal, powerless and vastly exploited. According to 1991 census, only 39 per cent of Indian women are literate, women's presence in the workforce is 14, and there are only 929 women to every 1,000 men. The use of amniocentesis has led to increase in female foeticide in the last decade. Besides infanticide, neglect of girl children, grossly inadequate health care account for this demographic disparity. Women remain more or less on the periphery of the political arena. At every level of the workforce, from wage labourer to highly paid professional, gender discrimination deprives her of opportunities, options and remuneration. Given the low level of education, they remain largely unaware of their rights under the law. Laws are either not implemented or are flouted with impunity.

The Indian feminist movement continues to seek legal remedies for social practices that specifically discriminate against and disadvantage women, such as widow immolation, dowry murders and harassment, while demanding equality in spheres of work and education.[32] But law has failed to protect her from violence.

Nehru himself admitted the limited role of law in fostering social changes when he declared at a joint sitting of both Houses of Parliament on the Dowry Prohibition Act in May, 1961: "Legislation cannot by itself normally solve deep-rooted social problems. One has to approach them in other ways too, but legislation is necessary and essential, so that it may give that push and have the educative factor as well as

32. Nair, Janaki, 1996, *Women and Law in Colonial India*, New Delhi: Kali for Women.

the legal sanctions behind which help public opinion to be given a certain shape."[33]

The Joint Committee of Parliament on DPA, in its report, referred to this limited role of legislation and stressed that laws can be effective only if backed by strong public opinion. It is therefore essential that social legislation must be widely published and public opinion properly educated with a view to ensure a reasonable and willing acceptance by the society. Laws can prove effective only if they are backed by major sections of the society.

Gandhiji once said: "A strong public opinion should be created in condemnation of the degraded practice of dowry and young men who soil their fingers with such illgotten gold should be excommunicated from the society." For he believed that "it is not legislation that will cure a popular ill, it is enlightened public opinion that can do it."[34]

During the debate on Dowry Prohibition Bill, members generally felt that the whole problem could be solved very easily and more quickly not by legislation but by rousing social conscience.[35] But the social conscience still appears in slumber as dowry deaths continue to rise, dowry demands keep escalating, and dowry advertisements keep appearing under the words "decent marriage".

---

33. Madhok, Alka, 1994, "Curbing Evils of Dowry", *Yojna*, Vol.58, No.16, September 15.
34. Hingorani, Anand,1964, *The Role of Women*, Bombay: Bhartiya Vidya Bhawan.
35. Sheel, Ranjana, 1999, *The Political Economy of Dowry Institutionalisation and Expansion in North India*, New Delhi: Manohar.

V

Public Opinion and Enactment of Laws in India

Hindu Code Bill

In western democracies, laws are generally passed in response to the prevailing majority opinion. That is not necessary the case in India and other developing countries. Legislators in India have sometimes been more progressive in social matters and ahead of the prevailing public opinion.[1]

The Constitution of India assigns to law a significant role in ushering in social change. By enacting social legislations, Indian Parliament sought to revolutionise the place of women in Indian society. Gandhiji for the first time highlighted the role of women in the major task of social reconstruction and nation building. He inspired them to participate in the national movement and gave them a new cause and a new sense

1. Tarkunde, V.M., 1976 "Social Justice and Law", *Monthly Public Opinion Surveys*, Vol. XXIII, No.9-10, June-July.

of commitment. However, he did not spell out any definite programme for women to achieve socio-economic equality. He did not attribute to law the capacity to give women self-esteem, rather he attributed to women's acquisition of self-esteem the capacity to change the law.[2]

For Nehru, participation of women in the national movement was the beginning of a larger social revolution, whereby women would struggle to find their proper identity in the Indian social milieu and enjoy equal rights with men. He believed that laws should be instruments of social change, which could break the socio-legal restraints on women and give them equal rights. In his words, "a society needed 'surgical operations' to effect radical social change. A majority in a democratic assembly by passing a law—a very advanced law—performs an operation like that."[3] Nehru was keen to liberate the Indian women through enactment of progressive social legislations. He visualised that education of public opinion would ultimately rally around support to get the measures of socio-legal equality between man and woman passed. This, however, was easier said than done, as it took Nehru several years before he finally realised the volume of orthodox opinion arranged against him in his bid to carry forward progressive legislation affecting personal laws.[4]

In the early years, Hindu law was unwritten and was governed by diversity of customs and commentators. The British

---

2. Levy, Harold, 1963, *Hindu Code Bill in British India* (A Dissertation for M.A.), Department of Political Science, Chicago: University of Chicago.
3. Menda, Tibor,1958, *Conversations with Nehru*, Bombay: Wilco Publishing House.
4. Som, Reba, 1994, "Jawaharlal Nehru and the Hindu Code: A Victory of Symbol Over Substance", *Modern Asian Studies*, New Delhi: Nehru Memorial Museum Library.

followed the policy of neutrality and non-interference in Hindu and Muslim laws and gave primacy to protecting imperial interests. Imposition of British jurisprudence therefore resulted not in the infusion of modern principles into traditional law but rather reformulation of traditional codes in an orthodox direction.[5] The attitude of colonial masters was largely that of non-interference in social customs. This led to complete stagnation in the prevailing legal system.

Realising that piecemeal legislation was not sufficient to meet the growing demands for modernising the whole structure of the law, the Government of India appointed a committee with B.N. Rau as the chairman to suggest changes and also to codify and unify the laws governing Hindus.[6]

In its first report, in 1941, the Rau Committee suggested a code which would be the blend of the finest elements in the various schools of Hindu law, would be simple in its language, capable of being translated into the vernacular and made accessible to all. In 1944, the Rau Committee submitted a draft which gave a widow the same share as a son in the husband's property and gave a daughter half a son's share; polygamy was banned; inter-caste marriage was legalised; and some divorce was made possible. The committee toured extensively and examined a large number of witnesses, most of whom opposed the code. The code's opponents mobilised demonstrations against it in five cities. Thus, the nationalist men supported the principle of sexual equality and its imple-

---

5. Forbes, Geraldine, 1984, "In Pursuit of Justice: Women's Organisation and Legal Reform", *Samya Shakti*, No.2, New Delhi: CWDS.
6. Sarkar, Lotika, "Jawaharlal Nehru and the Hindu Code Bill", in Nanda, B.R., (ed.), 1976, *Indian Women: From Purdah to Modernity*, New Delhi: Vikas.

mentation through women's suffrage, which undermined Britain's position of power. But they opposed the principle in marriage and inheritance, which threatened the privileges of the men in the family.[7] Significant steps could not be taken following the submission of the draft till after independence, because of the hostile public opinion.

Immediately after independence, under Nehru's leadership, the draft code was referred to a Select Committee under the chairmanship of the Law Minister, Dr. B.R. Ambedkar. While introducing the code in the Constituent Assembly, Ambedkar pointed out that the main aim of the bill was to codify the rules of the Hindu law which are scattered in innumerable decisions of the High Courts and the Privy Council, which form a bewildering motely to the common man.[8] One of the most important provisions of the code, he said, was the provision relating to 'dowry' which, as then prevalent, was a "scandalous affair which not only lowered the dignity of the woman but to her being often subject to both physical and mental oppression". He pointed out that the suggestion of making this into a trust property for the girl would go a long way in improving the situation. This bill raised the age of consent and marriage, upheld monogamy, treated dowry as stridhan or women's property. The members of the Constituent Assembly vehemently opposed the Hindu Code Bill which, they felt was an attempt at demolition of the entire structure and fabric of the Hindu society.[9]

In the immediate post-independence period, public atti-

---

7. Liddle, J., Joshi, R., 1986, *Daughters of Independence: Gender, Caste and Class in India*, New Delhi: Kali for Women.
8. *Constituent Assembly Debates* (CAD), 1948, Vol.V, April 9, New Delhi: Government of India.
9. *CAD*, 1949, Vol.VII, Part II, December.

tudes towards the bill had become negative for several reasons. The violence of partition had made the orthodox, Hindu politicians strive for a Hindu Raj where Hindu values would be central. One of Rau committee members D.N. Mitter's lengthy note of dissent to the Rau Committee report in 1947 rallied bill opponents. Mitter had objected to the Code as an imitation of western ideas inferior to and destructive of Hindu ideals and culture, especially in regard to women. The position of Ambedkar as untouchable and as Law Minister reforming Hindu law provoked further opposition. Opponents of the bill argued that the women assembly members were not representing the general women's opinion, and that the reformers were influenced by western education and law, instead of Hinduism and were unpatriotic. The opponents claimed that bill were against Hindu religion and society and would destroy the cohesion of the Hindu family and lead to fragmentation of family assets. They asserted that men's and women's obligations were different, which made it unfair for men and women to have the same property rights.

Conflict over the bill existed within the top ranks of Congress leadership after independence. Gandhiji had supported efforts to improve women's status, but he was opposed to legalistic approaches to social issues. Nehru strongly supported the bill but all other top Congress leaders like Dr. Rajendra Prasad (Congress President 1947-48, and President of India, 1950-61), Vallabh bhai Patel (Home Minister until his death in 1950), B. Pattabhai Sitaramayya (Congress President,1948-50), and Purshottam Das Tandon (Congress President in 1950) opposed the bill. Dr. Rajendra Prasad held that the code had not sufficiently been discussed, circulated and presented for public opinion. Age-old traditions could not be brushed aside by hastily enacted legislations. Congress President Pattabhi Sitaramayya warned that the bill would replace the socialistic structure of the joint family within an alien individualistic civilisation. Dr. Rajendra Prasad intimated that he might assert the authority to veto the bill for lack of a specific mandate.[10] He admonished that the code be deferred until after the election, which led Nehru to abandon the bill until after the first general election in 1952. Ambedkar resigned in protest.

The supporters of the bill argued within the discourse of equal rights insisting that equality within the public sphere be extended to the family. Many women members of parliament as well as the Congress like Renuka Ray, Durgabai Deshmukh and Sucheta Kriplani argued that political equality was meaningless without economic and social equality provided by female inheritance rights. The supporters endorsed that these principles were not foreign, but formed part of the heritage of the nationalist movement. However, the justification of Hindu law reform on the basis of liberal egalitarian principles provoked much societal hostility as they appeared alien to Hindu tradition.

Women members failed to recognise that "the politics of pleas, prayers and petitions without the backing of a broad based social movement, could produce only limited effects."[11]

A difficulty encountered by women's movement in India, has been its liability to mobilise large number of people. Indian women's movement failed to mobilise the mass opinion

---

10. President Rajendra Prasad's note to Nehru, 14 September, 1951, Munshi, K.M., 1967, *Indian Constitutional Documents, Pilgrimage to Freedom*, Vol. 1, Bombay: Bhartiya Vidya Bhawan.
11. Nair, Janaki, 1996, *Women and Law in Colonial India: A Social History*, New Delhi: Kali for Women.

in favour of Hindu Code Bill.[12]

Hindu Code Bill was eventually treated in a piecemeal fashion. It was split into five parts and made more acceptable by whittling down the controversial points. Even then it took a few years before the Hindu Marriage Act was passed in 1955, followed by the Hindu Succession Act, the Hindu Minority and Guardianship Act and the Hindu Adoption and Maintenance Act, all of which were passed in 1956, and finally the Dowry Prohibition Act in 1961. Sardar Hukum Singh's statement is relevant: "It is not the public opinion that has changed its attitude. This is not the original bill. That Hindu Code had practically been given up by the government."[13] Nehru had to dilute substantially his original position, resulting in a set of legislation which was more symbolic than substantial in character. Nehru began with the vision of a Uniform Civil Code but ended by accepting the diluted version of a truncated Hindu Code. For him it was not however a surrender of principles but merely the pragmatic recognition of the volume of opposition that pitted against him.[14] While Nehru decided to play in tune with the mass opinion, Ambedkar was keen to override the hostile public opinion, holding that parliament would not be able to function if it had to be subject everytime to the vote of the ignorants, people outside who do not know the elementary facts of law making.[15]

From 1947 to 1960, the founding generation of the In-

---

12. Everett, J.M., 1981, *Women and Social Change in India*, New Delhi: Heritage Publishers.
13. *Lok Sabha Debates* (LSD), 1954, Vol. V, Part II, pp. 7253-4.
14. Som, R., supra note 4.
15. Ambedkar, B.R., *Parliamentary Debates* (PD), 6, ii, 51, col. 2467, Parashar, A., (ed.), 1992, *Women and Family Law: Reform in India*, New Delhi: Sage.

dian Constitution had relative autonomy of leadership and exercised relatively greater hold over the public opinion. Nehru's victory over P. D. Tandon gave him an autonomous space.

But even the founding generation of liberal modernist forces led by Nehru were reluctant to initiate changes which would shake up the social fabric too drastically. He held: "We may pass the bill in spite of this opposition, but there would be great obstruction in the implementation of the bill when passed. Large number of people might offer this obstruction in an organised way. It is always difficult to deal with this kind of thing."[16]

Nehru was far ahead of public opinion as far as the Hindu Code Bill was concerned. He had to ultimately submit to the majority opinion. The Congress old guards succeeded in slowing him down in his bid to bring about social reform through the instrument of law. What was passed merely codified a woman's secondary status in the society. The opposition from the die-hards was so strong that some of the basic inequalities rooted in the joint family system and the personal inheritance laws could not be removed. The orthodox opinion was thus placated and compromised. The half-hearted approach revealed the patriarchal state's compulsions, ambivalence and the lack of will to make social justice a reality.[17]

The very same political actors who had agreed to those equality rights within the public sphere, a few years earlier, fiercely resisted the effort to renegotiate the boundaries be-

16. Jawaharlal Nehru to Ambedkar, 26 February 1945, in S. Gopal, (ed.), 1972, *Selected Works of J. L. Nehru*, New Delhi, second series, Vol.10, Oxford University Press.
17. Sheel, Ranjana, 1999, *The Political Economy of Dowry, Institutionalisation and Expansion in North India*, New Delhi: Manohar.

tween the public and private. The idea of woman as full and equal participants in the political and economic spheres carried the day. But the idea of women as full and equal participants in the domestic sphere was simply too radical. The discourse of equality was not able to successfully challenge and displace the ideological construction of women as wives and mothers within the family.[18]

Anti-Dowry Laws

The attempts to reform the Hindu law evoked strong protest from the orthodox sections steeped in patriarchy. They succeeded in stalling the Hindu Code Bill. The hold of tradition was so strong that some glaring features of discrimination against women remained. This was most marked in the law dealing with inheritance. In spite of the loud proclamation of the principle of equality between the sexes, Mitakshara coparcenary, giving preferential rights to sons in the joint family property, was retained. The daughter was also denied a share in the dwelling house, and only a right of residence to the unmarried or in-distress daughter was provided for. Powers of testation were also kept unlimited, often used as a device to disinherit women heirs. The orthodox opinion, favoured limitation of women's rights in property to rights over '*stridhana*' as well as gifts given at the time of marriage. With the passing of the the Hindu Succession Act, 1956, declaring in principle equal inheritance for men and women, the notion of '*stridhana*' as women's separate property appears redundant and with little justification. It assumes that a woman loses the membership of her parental family after marriage. It provides an easy avenue for the in-law's family to appropri-

18. Kapur, Ratna and Crossman, Brenda, 1996, *Subversive Sites Feminist Engagement with Law in India*, New Delhi: Sage.

ate. This concept was central to the arguments that favoured gift giving to the bride at the time of marriage and has acted as the chief motivating factor for the institution of modern dowry.

The Dowry Prohibition Act, 1961 was promulgated as an acknowledgement of dowry as a major social evil. Members of parliament recognised that dowry was all pervasive phenomenon and must be uprooted.[19]

Attempts to control dowry through mechanism of the law dates as far back as the Sind Leti Deti Act of 1939. Following independence, only two states, namely, Bihar and Andhar Pradesh enacted legislation for restraining the taking or giving of dowry in marriage. But as incidence of dowry escalated, need for central legislation was felt and the first systematic law to prohibit dowry known as the Dowry Prohibition Act was passed in 1961. However, the Act proved quite ineffective and limited.

In the parliamentary debates preceding the bill, the attempt to delink gift giving with marriage was spurned by 99 per cent of the participating MPs.[20]

Some members regarded dowry as an ancient custom which had provided 'security' and 'protection' to women. As such it was a mark of affection for the daughter.[21] Dowry as such was not an evil till the demands went beyond the reasonable financial competence of the bride's party.[22] No radical reform was apparently acceptable to the members. In

---

19. *Lok Sabha Debate* (LSD), 1959:4436.
20. Ibid., 3441.
21. Illa, Palchowdhary, (LSD-3437), Lakshmi Bai of Vikarabad, (LSD 3758-59), Manjula Devi of Gopalpara, (LSD-3701-2), etc.
22. LSD, 3445-51.

fact it was felt that marriage, which is the starting point for a girl's life, must be accompanied by gift giving.[23] Dowry was even justified for ensuring daughter's economic independence and security in life.[24] Only when the money is extorted, or any property is extorted as a consideration, would it come under the preview of the act. Of course some members like Parvati Krishnan, Subhadra Joshi, Renu Chakravarty demanded the delinking of marriage with gift giving in order to end the exploitation of women.

In fact, most of the discussion focussed on the scope of dowry or on what was permissible. There was no attempt to declare dowry as an illegal custom. Thus, there were many suggestions to limit the value of customary presentations made at the time of marriage to the bride and the groom. In fact, Menon pointed out that to permit gift giving according to custom would only legalise dowry.[25]

The Speaker as well as A.K. Sen, the Law Minister, on the other hand upheld customary gift giving, but condemned dowry which was extortion.[26]

Finally, the clause 2, i.e., the definition of dowry, as present in the Dowry Prohibition Act, 1961, was passed with 183 members approving and 40 voting against it. The Act laid down a very narrow definition of dowry as "property given in consideration of marriage and as a condition of the marriage taking place." The definition excluded presents in the form of cash, ornaments, clothes and other articles from its purview. The definition also did not cover any money asked for and given after marriage.

---

23. LSD, 3454.
24. LSD, 3702.
25. LSD, 3964.
26. LSD, 3966-67.

Thus, the state's major aim and objectives in the presentation of the Dowry Prohibition Act was not the complete abolition of the practice but to maintain it within tolerable limits in the patriarchal social structure, of which the state itself was an integral part.[27]

Majority of the members were opposed to making dowry a cognisable offence as it would lead to police entering the privacy of family.[28] Clause 8 was finally adopted as part of the bill which left the dowry offence as non cognisable, bailable and non-compoundable. In other words, taking of dowry was treated as a trivial offence.

Further, both giving and taking of dowry was made an offence under the Act. The maximum punishment was six months and/or a fine of Rs. 5,000. To make matters more complicated, prior sanction of the government was necessary for prosecuting a husband who demanded dowry. Complaints had to be filed within a year of the offence and only by the aggrieved person. This again was unpractical and unrealistic as they were unwilling to lodge a complaint for fear of it affecting their daughter adversely. In fact, the members had little faith in the legal enactment and hoped that social awakening and a strong public opinion could prevent the law from coming in fruition.[29]

Dowry problem was viewed in itself and not in its large context of women's subordination or their deteriorating status. Problem of dowry is likely to remain unabated within the framework of a patriarchal state and society.[30]

---

27. Sheel, Ranjana, supra note 17.
28. LSD, 3437, 3770.
29. LSD, 3715.
30. Sheel, R., supra note 17.

Thus, the members were not opposed to dowry as an ancient custom providing security to the girl, constituting daughter's share of property. They favoured dowry that was willing and affectionately given and were against demands that were to be forcibly extracted. Hence, the Dowry Prohibition Act, 1961 did not ban dowry completely but tried to keep it within reasonable limits.

Ineffectiveness of the Dowry Prohibition Act, 1961

The Dowry Prohibition Act remained largely ineffective. This is manifested at different levels.

First, there were hardly cases filed under this Act and there were less than half a dozen convictions in the period between the enactment and the amendment. The enactment failed to have a deterrent effect. Dowry was no longer confined to demands made and met at the time of marriage but became a continuous demand at festivals, childbirth or even to finance the son-in-law's business or education abroad. In total defiance of the Act, the dowry custom percolated down to all other communities and areas which had hitherto not practised it earlier.

The demand for changing this toothless piece of legislation was first made in the report of the Committee on the Status of Women in India,[31] and later through strong women's movement all over the country. With a view to remedy the inherent weakness of the Dowry Prohibition Act, a private bill was introduced in the parliament by Smt. Pramila Dandavate, MP on June 13, 1980. The bill was considered and the question of working of Dowry Prohibition Act, 1961

31. *Towards Equality: Report of the Committee on the Status of Women in India*, New Delhi: Government of India, 1974.

was referred to the Joint Parliamentary Committee (JPC), which attributed the failure of Act to the following reasons:

First, gift giving permitted by Act nullified the objective of the Act.

Secondly, the Act lacked enforcement, as the parents of the victim were unwilling to lodge a complaint because of the fear that their daughter could be victimised.

The JPC noted with concern that dowry had assumed grotesque and alarming proportions. Education had increased the demand for dowry both in rural and urban areas. Although dowry on theoretical plane is condemned by all in this country, in actual life most of them are parties to this vice. The JPC felt that laws can prove effective only if they are backed by major sections of the society. Two conditions need to be satisfied: there must be a favourable social climate in support of that law, and the administrative willingness to implement that law.

The JPC made certain significant recommendations in this regard:

(1) The words "in consideration for the marriage" ought to be deleted from the definition of dowry.

(2) It sought to introduce a ceiling in respect of the gifts given as well as the expenses incurred for the wedding. Gifts given to the bride should be listed and registered in her name and in the event of the bride's death, should revert back to her parents and in the event of divorce, to her. It must be ensured that gifts remain exclusively for the bride's benefit.

(3) Giver of the dowry, i.e., bride's parents, should not be equated with those who take dowry. Only those who take

or abet the taking of dowry should be punished. Punishment should be deterrent and fine adequate.

(4) Dowry Prohibition Officers should be appointed for the enforcement of the Act.

(5) The offences under the Act should be made cognisable, subject to the condition that no arrest shall be made by the police officer without a warrant or an order of the magistrate. The committee believed that if loopholes are plugged, implementation is strict, punishment is made deterrent and public is properly educated, the dowry prohibition law would bring about the desired results.[32]

It was only after pressure from the women's movement that the Joint Parliamentary Committee's report was tabled in the parliament. Thus effective public pressure led the Government to enact Dowry Prohibition Amendment Act, 1984. The Act substituted the words in "connection with marriage" for the words "as consideration for the marriage". Presents should be of a customary nature, not of an excessive value and were to be listed. The amendment recognised the need to make the offence cognisable for the purpose of investigation. It increased punishment to five years and a fine upto Rs.10,000 or the value of dowry, whichever is more. It also removed one year limitation period. It extended the right to recognise women's organisations and welfare institutions to initiate proceedings in a court. It removed the requirement of prior sanction of the government for prosecuting a husband who demands dowry.

The suggestion of imposing a ceiling on gifts and mar-

---

32. Report of the Joint Parliamentary Committee to examine the question of the working of the Dowry Prohibition Act, 1961 (August 10, 1982).

riage expenditure did not find a place in the Act.

The Act was again amended in 1986 to make its provisions more stringent and also to make its implementation effective. The fine was increased to Rs.15,000. The burden of proving offence was shifted to the accused. All dowry offences were made non-bailable. Advertisements offering dowry in consideration for marriage were made punishable. The state governments were empowered to appoint Dowry Prohibition Officers and Advisory Boards. A new section on 'dowry death' was introduced in the Indian Penal Code (Section 304B) and whosoever is found of committing dowry death shall be punished with imprisonment for not less than seven years, extendible to life imprisonment (Section 498A). Sections 113A and 113B of the Indian Evidence Act lay down presumptive rule of evidence in favour of the prosecution.

In wake of the recommendations made by the 91st report of the Law Commission in August 1983, these changes were introduced in the Indian Penal Code, 1860, Criminal Procedure Code, 1973 and the Evidence Act, 1872 to deal more effectively with dowry deaths and cruelty to married women. For violence at home, behind closed doors, by close relatives had to be dealt on a different plane. For direct evidence is hard to find and where the success or failure of the prosecution depends on the adequacy of circumstantial evidence. Section 304B of Indian Penal Code relates to dowry death. Section 498A of Indian Penal Code defines cruelty and deals with cruelty of husband and his relatives. The Indian Evidence Act was amended to shift the burden of proof on the husband and his family. Through amendment in Criminal Procedure Code, a provision was made for inquest by Executive Magistrate and for post-mortem in all cases where a woman has, within seven years of her marriage, committed suicide, or died in suspicious circumstances.

All these amendments tried to strengthen the enforcement machinery to curb the menace of dowry deaths.

Escalation of Dowry Violence Despite Laws

Continuing frequency of dowry deaths is the evidence of the powerless position of women in Indian society. Dowry violence is a matter of exploiting unequal power relationship in a family. With all the amendments in procedural and substantive law, the evil of dowry continues unabated. These laws do not seem to have helped women to get justice. Despite all these legal measures, there is an alarming rise in dowry deaths. According to the National Crime Records Bureau, 1994, 4,215 dowry deaths were reported in 1989, which went upto 4,836 in 1990, 5,157 in 1991, came down slightly to 4,962 in 1992 and rose to 5,817 in 1993, and 5,199 in 1994. Thus approximately 6,000 dowry deaths take place in India every year. It may be said that a dowry death takes place every 90 minutes. In reality the unreported deaths are even higher.

Failure of the Enforcement Machinery

There is often a wide gap between the legislative intent and use of laws and legal processes in reality.[33] Lack of sensitivity and concern on the part of the enforcement machinery has chiefly contributed to the failure of the Dowry Prohibition Act. Police has often played a negative role in dowry deaths, have appeared unconcerned, hesitated and refused to register a case as murder and tend to look upon them as domestic dispute or cases of suicides. Often when a woman goes to a

33. National Perspective Plan for Women 1988-2000 A.D., 1988, *Introduction*, pp. XII, New Delhi: Government of India.

police station to lodge a complaint against her violent husband, invariably the police instead of writing down the complaint gives her a moral discourse on how she should behave.[34] Investigations are conducted in an extremely casual and unscientific manner. Post-morterms are not held and if they arc held evidence is easily tampered with. Often police appear in collusion with the culprits. Insufficient and careless investigation by the police often results in acquittal.[35] Police malfunctioning and apathy has taken many forms, among them undue influence in recording dying declarations, delay in sending the body for postmortem, intimidation of prime witnesses and exploitation of the legal ignorance of both parties to extort money as a price to build a good case in their favour.

The role of the administrative machinery in the implementation of the anti-dowry law is equally to be found wanting. As administrative agents, government doctors, prosecutors and Dowry Prohibition Officers are often found guilty of professional misconduct. Collusion with the interest party is not unusual.

Although an increase in the number of dowry death cases is evident, only a tiny proportion are reported, of which fewer still reach trial and judgement. Statistics compiled by the National Crime Records Bureau (1995) reveals that as many as 87.1 per cent of the dowry death cases remained pending in the courts as compared to the disposal rate of

---

34. *Saheli*, 1988, see, chapter entitled, "Policing the Police".
35. Kumari, Ranjana, 1989, *Brides are Not for Burning: Dowry Victims in India*, New Delhi: Radiant; Chauhan, Richa, 1995, *Dowry in the Twentieth Century India: A Window to the Conflict of Caste, Class and Gender* (Dissertation in Sociology), Stony Brook: State University of New York.

12.9 per cent in the year 1995. This may be due partly to the lengthy and archaic judicial procedure. More alarming is the extremely low rate of conviction. The acquittal or discharge in cases of cruelty by the husband or his relatives amounted to 75.8 per cent (National Crime Records Bureau, 1995).

In Bhagwant Singh v Commissioner of Police case, the Supreme Court lamented upon the fact that the police did not display the promptitude and efficiency which the investigation of the case required.[36]

In dowry cases, the attitude of the judiciary has been ambivalent and inconsistent to say the least.[37] The record of the court documents reflects the failure of the legal system to improve society and to protect women. In fact judiciary is not free from gender bias. Cumbersome court procedure and overcrowding of cases hamper their speedy disposal. The attitude of the judiciary at the lower level is to dismiss most of the cases on grounds of insufficient evidence. Thus for women, litigation does not guarantee justice.[38] Certain cases may be cited, illustrating the amibivalent attitude of the judiciary, brought up in the traditional norms of our society.

In Sudha Goel dowry death case[39] on May 27, 1983, in his historic judgment, the Additional Sessions Judge (ADJ) of Delhi, S.M. Agarwal sentenced to death, the husband, brother-in-law and mother-in-law of Sudha Goel. He also passed severe strictures on the police and the doctor and described the murder as gruesome and diabolic.

---

36. 1983 (3) SCC 344.
37. Sarkar, L., 1995, "Women's Movement and the Legal Process", Occasional Paper, No.24, New Delhi: CWDS.
38. Gonsalves, Lina, 1993, *Women And Law*, New Delhi: Lancer.
39. 1985(4)SCC 476.

However, the death sentence given by the ADJ was reversed by the High Court, dismissing all charges against the accused. This was described by media as a 'shocking verdict', a "legal sanction to dowry". Eleven women's organisations and groups submitted a joint appeal in the Supreme Court against the judgment. While agreeing with the view that bride burning was serious enough to merit a death sentence, the Supreme Court justified reducing it to a life sentence on the ground that the accused had been acquitted and there had been a lapse of two years, since the acquittal. The husband, while out on bail, married again and even had two children before he went into jail to complete a term for life. Thus, it is extremely easy for the husband, charged with the murder of his first wife, to get married to another woman.

In Wazir Chand v Haryana case[40], the young daughter-in-law Veena died of burn injuries. On the basis of the evidence, the ADJ as well as the Punjab and Haryana High Courts convicted the husband and the father-in-law under section 306 (abatement to suicide) and section 498A (cruelty by husband or relatives) of the IPC, and sentenced them to three years and fine for the first offence and one year imprisonment and fine for the second offence. However, the Supreme Court, on appeal, sentenced the father-in-law and the husband for the offence under section 498A and confirmed the sentence of the of the sessions court of one year's rigorous imprisonment and a fine of Rs.100. This clearly indicates that demand for dowry and harassment are being treated as minor offences not meriting severe punishment but merely one year imprisonment and a paltry fine. Dowry deaths, when proved, ought to deserve the highest punishment under law.

---

40. *All India Reporter*, (AIR), 1989, SC 378.

Similarly, in the Gurbachan Singh v Satpal Singh case[41], the young woman died of burns within seven months of her marriage. She was not only harassed by constant demands for things but mentally tortured by the insinuation that the child she was carrying was illegitimate. The sessions court held the in-laws guilty of abatement of suicide and therefore punishable under section 306 of the IPC.

On an appeal to the High Court the conviction was reversed and benefit of doubt was given to the in-laws. But, on appeal, the Supreme Court reversed the High Court judgment and restored the order of conviction by the sessions judge. The case reveals the inconsistent attitude of the judiciary.

Male bias of the judges in the lower courts is evident in Ashok Kumar v State of Rajasthan case.[42] The sessions judge decided to ignore the dying declaration of the doctors that she had been burnt by her brother-in-law. Instead he decided to acquit the accused on the very flimsy ground that there was a contradiction between the two doctors, one of whom was a woman. However, the verdict was reversed by the High Court, whose judgment Supreme Court also confirmed. It is necessary to record the judge was uncharitable in discarding the testimony (of the doctor) and doubting her truthfulness principally because she was a woman forgetting she was a doctor of 14 years standing.

Lichhamandevi v State of Rajasthan[43] is another case of insufficient dowry brought by the bride which led to her

41. AIR, 1990, SC 209.
42. AIR, 1990, SC 2134.
43. AIR, 1988, SC 1785.

death at the hands of the in-laws. An over-domineering mother-in-law harassed the daughter-in-law, Pushpa, and her son remained a mute spectator to all harassments and cruelty to his wife. Finally, one day the mother-in-law having poured kerosene on her daughter-in- law, set her on fire. This was confirmed by Pushpa in her statement to the doctor and the investigating officer. The trial court acquitted the mother-in-law. The High Court reversed the verdict to one of death penalty. The Supreme Court reduced the High Court's sentence to that of life imprisonment cautioning that judge's decisions should not be swayed by anger or emotions. On what basis the sessions judge had acquitted the mother-in-law in such a dastardly and diabolic murder is not clear.

All murders of young women by their husbands or in-laws are euphemistically called dowry deaths and not murder. The facts in Subedar Tiwari v State of Uttar Pradesh[44] were revolting. Veena, an M.Sc. in Botany with a brilliant record, was married to a doctor. Discovering his illicit relationship she planned to take up a job and leave him, when the tragic incident of her being burnt to death in a flat in the placid campus of Banaras Hindu University took place. The trial court convicted the husband and his sister Meera under sections 302 and 34 of IPC and sentenced the former to death and latter to life imprisonment. On appeal, the Allahabad High Court set aside the order of conviction, holding that suicide could not be ruled out. Later, on an appeal to the Supreme Court, the court sentenced the husband to life imprisonment for murder of his wife but did not wish to interfere with the acquittal of the sister.

---

44. 1988(2) SCALE 1341: Sarkar, Lotika, "Women and Law", *Annual Survey of Indian Law*, 1988, New Delhi: Indian Law Institute.

Again, in Brij Lal v Prem Chand case[45], Veena Rani was murdered by her advocate husband. The ADJ found the accused guilty under section 306 and convicted him to four years rigourous imprisonment. But High Court acquitted the accused. But, the Supreme Court found the judgment of the High Court unsustainable and suffering from serious errors and infirmities.

The courts have often resorted to soft justice in fixing the punishment of those guilty of perpetuating dowry deaths.

In the Manjushree Sarda case,[46] the Pune sessions court convicted the husband of murdering his wife by poisoning. The Bombay High Court upheld the conviction. But when the husband went in appeal to the Supreme Court, the judgment of the lower courts was reversed and the husband was acquitted. This case also raised a public debate. The judges of the apex court in the country not only ignored facts like the husband's knowledge of chemicals, his relationship with another woman, and evidence of cruel treatment meted out to the wife but reversed the High Court's death sentence by adhering to their theories of psychotic behaviour and depression leading to suicide.

In another hotly debated case,[47] the wife Vibha Shukla was found burnt while the husband Ashok Shukla, was pre-

---

45. AIR, 1989, SC, 1661, quoted in Sivaramayya, B., "Women and the Law", *Annual Survey of Indian Law*, 1988, New Delhi: Indian Law Institute.
46. Sharad Sarda vs. State of Maharashtra, 1986, *Criminal Law Journal*; Agnes, F., "Violence Against Women: Review of Recent Enactment", Mukhopadhyay, S., (ed.), 1998, *In the Name of Justice*, New Delhi: Manohar.
47. State of Maharashtra vs. Ashok Chhotelal Shukla-Bombay High Court Judgment dated 14 January, 1986, AIR, 1997, SC 3111.

sent in the house. A huge amount of dowry was paid at the time of the wedding and there were several subsequent demands for dowry. Vibha's father-in-law was a senior police officer in Bombay. When Vibha had delivered a daughter, their family did not accept the child, who was left behind at her parents house. The Bombay High Court set aside the conviction of the sessions court acquitting the husband of the charge of murder and harassment under section 498A of IPC. For occasional cruelty and harassment could not be constructed as cruelty under section 498A of IPC according to the High Court. This is a case of the court siding with the influential and powerful elites.

Geeta Gandhi's killers, her husband and father-in-law, were acquitted by the Bombay High Court presuming that Geeta might have committed suicide because of depression caused by her ill-health.[48]

In Shobha Rani v Madhulkar Reddi case,[49] the husband and his parents made demands for money from the wife. She went to court for divorce or ground of cruelty. The trial court in Andhra held that there is nothing strange in his (husband's) asking his wife for money when he is in need of it. The High Court also found it quite understandable and natural when a husband asks his rich wife to give him some money for his personal use, the wife must extend all help, it said. The Supreme Court having examined all the evidence drew a distinction between a husband or a wife asking the other spouse for some money and harassing a wife to bring more

48. Dilip Kumar Tarachand Gandhi & Anr. vs. State of Maharashtra, Bombay High Court Judgment dated 6 March,1991 in Criminal Appeal 51 of 1991, cited by Sethi N. & Anand K.,1988, "A Life of Humiliation, *Manushi*, 45.

49. AIR, 1988, SC 121.

because her parents were rich. The apex court categorically rejected the stand of the lower courts and held there was a demand for dowry and entitled the wife to get a divorce on the ground of cruelty. What is significant is that the trial court and the High Court justified the demands for money because after all the young wife was a rich woman.

In State v Udham Singh case, a young woman Shanni Kaur died of burns in a Delhi hospital. Before dying she gave her statement three times, once to the police and twice to different doctors, stating that her husband had burnt her. All the three declarations were discounted in the court. Dowry murders occur within the four walls of the home, and there is no evidence against the men as the offence committed is beyond the public gaze. But even in cases where there is evidence, the courts chose not to believe the women, even her dying declaration is discredited[50] Often out of fear or social stigma the dying woman exonerates her husband or in-laws of burning her.

Thus, judiciary is not free from gender bias. The bias in dowry deaths and wife burning cases is obvious from the low conviction rate of the accused as the cases are usually dismissed as suicides or accidents. Though sometimes progressive judgments have been delivered, by and large judiciary is dominated by men and is biased in favour of men. In fact the vigorous women's movement and pressure exerted by women's organisations have been chiefly responsible for reversal of anti-women judgments by courts. Often husbands and in-laws have been acquitted by the courts. The entrenched values of some of our judges which believes in male superiority and the subordinate position of women, makes them often forget the constitutional mandate of equality of

---

50. Gonslaves, Lina, 1993, supra note 38.

sexes or the international campaign for human rights for both men and women.[51]

S.M. Aggarwal, Additional Sessions Judge of Delhi (who came to limelight when he awarded death sentence to the accused in the Sudha Goel case), called for a change in the law to prohibit for at least five years the remarriage of a man whose wife had died under suspicious circumstances. Aggarwal also cautioned the police not to take at face value a woman's dying statement exonerating her in-laws.

In Indersen v State of Bihar case[52] and in Kashi Prasad v State of Bihar case,[53] the Patna High Court expressed the view that mere demand for dowry would not constitute an offence under the section unless it was shown that the other party consented to pay it. Again in Inder Sain v Sinte case,[54] Luthra J. of the Delhi High Court observed that only those articles could be dowry which were given or were agreed to be given as reward or reason or motive for the solemnisation of marriage. Hence articles demanded after marriage was not dowry, though demands and maltreatment of the bride continued and finally she was turned out of the house. Similarly, Bombay High Court[55] in L.V. Jadhav v Shanker Rao case, in which though the in-laws had demanded Rs. 50,000 for the transport of the couple to the USA, held that since the demand for dowry was not accepted by the other party, no offence of demanding dowry was constituted. His view was however rejected by the Supreme Court. Such narrow inter-

---

51. Sarkar, L., 1995, supra note 37.
52. 1981, *Criminal Law Journal*, 116.
53. 1980, BBCJ 612.
54. Inder Sain vs Sinte, 1988, *Criminal Law Journal*, 116.
55. AIR, 1983, SC, 1219.

pretation by the courts defeated the very purpose of Dowry Prohibition Act 1961. Now ofcourse, if demand is made after the marriage, it would constitute demand for dowry. This was the view taken by P.K. Bahari in Harbans Singh v Guruchanran Kaur.[56]

The apex court has often played a dynamic role in expounding law and clarifying legal norms so that culprits do not escape because of the inadequacies and procedural technicalities of law. Such judgments (Pratibha Rani v Sushil Kumar, AIR 1985 SC 628; Surinder Kumar v State, AIR 1987, SC 386, State v Laxman, AIR 1986 SC 250, Brij Lal v Prem Chand, AIR 1989 SC 1661, Paniben (1992) 2 SCCD 474 and Ganeshlal v State of Maharashtra (1992) 3 SCC 106), though encouraging, only comprise a very small percentage of the total cases coming to trial. Evidence is still predominantly in favour of acquittal. Arbitrary and blatantly biased judicial strategies still operate at the level of subordinate courts. A lengthy and tedious court process often end in acquittal of the accused on flimsy grounds which leave little room for justice and fair play.[57]

Thus legislation alone is not enough to change centuries old customs and social taboos, but more than the law, what is required is to bring about a change in the attitudes of the legal agents—the police, the public prosecutors and judges.

Social Opinion and Dowry

Dowry, a form of marriage payment in Indian society, though

56. 1990, *Criminal Law Journal*, 1591.
57. Chowdhury, Manjaree, "Miles to go: An assessment of the enforcement hurdles in the implementation of the anti-dowry laws in India", Werner, Menski, (ed.), 1999, *South Asians and the Dowry Problem*, New Delhi: Vistar.

legally proscribed and publicly condemned, is still a culturally approved and socially sanctioned practice.[58]

Dowry is regarded as a normal practice, an accepted norm, a traditional custom. Legislation alone does not alter attitudes, or change centuries old customs and mores. Traditionally, an Indian woman is conditioned to accept an inferior role, to see herself as a dependent. Her socialisation prevents her from revolting against the family. The culture of silence keeps the oppressive marriage going at all costs. Marriage being the most important goal, parents of the girl are not interested in punishment of the offenders but the continuation of marriage which is considered sacred. They appear desperate to get their daughters married and keep them in their husband's home at all costs. Parents often discourage daughters from leaving tyrannical husbands. They prefer to put huge amount of money in the hands of a man who tortures her than to spend a small sum of the money in enabling her to survive independently.[59]

Parents have generally displayed a reactionary and conservative approach to marriage. They would not spend money on educating their daughters, or making them independent, but would spend huge sums of money on lavish weddings in the hope that the girl would never return to the native home and become a stigma.

A movement for protecting women's rights cannot align itself with parents who would go to any extent to disinherit their daughters, deprive them of education and equal oppor-

58. Government of India, 1974; Indian Institute of Public Opinion, 1978.
59. Kishwar, M., 1986, "Dowry To Ensure Her Happiness or To Disinherit her ?", *Manushi*, No.34.

tunities in life under the pretext of preserving the family honour, force them in marriage alliances for their own vested interests, or worse, willingly kill their daughters even before they are born in order to save the expenses of their marriage later in life.[60]

Dowry demands often go unreported as women fear that reporting may aggravate domestic violence or result in the breakdown of the marriage. The victim feels helpless and vulnerable. Young women are still generally compelled to put up with continuous atrocities because of deeply ingrained subservience to customs and mortifying fear of the stigma of single existence in an inflexible and dogmatic society (Grover, 1990).

Dowry is publicly condemned but privately practised. Dowry persists in social thinking. The Committee on the Status of Women in India, 1974, noted that "the educated youth is grossly insensitive to the evil of dowry and unashamedly contributes, to its perpetuation". Anna Mathews[61] has shown that because of the rise in material aspirations and expectations, youth seem to have come to depend heavily on the institution of dowry. One would expect enlightened and educated youth to reject the unethical and exploitative practice of dowry. Instead we find educated young men insisting on fabulous sums of money as bridegroom price and in almost all cases, the amount of dowry is regulated by the educational qualifications of the bridegroom and his eco-

60. Agnes, Flavia, "Violence Against Women: Review of Recent Enactments", in Mukhopadhyaya, S., (ed.), 1998, *In the Name of Justice*, New Delhi: Manohar.
61. Mathew, Anna, 1987, "Attitudes Towards Dowry", *The Indian Journal of Social Work*, Vol. XLVIII , No.1, April.

nomic status and prestige.[62]

The belief that the problem of dowry can be solved by making women economically independent is not true, as proved by a number of empirical studies. Unless the value system in favour of dowry is changed, the problem would persist. M.K. Sandhu's study[63] noticed that in the case of working women 86.7 per cent reported that dowry was given in marriage. Saroja Krishnaswamy's study[64] reveals that education, income and employment of women do not change their attitudes towards dowry. In fact the materialistic values, dominating the social scene, at present, have a dominating influence on the attitude and behaviour of the people. Modernisation has given rise to consumerist culture, where status is acquired in terms of luxury gadgets and electronic items one possesses. Employed women unknowingly become promoters of materialism.[65] Dowry is a malignant symptom

---

62. Rao, V.V.P. and Rao, V.N., 1980, "The Dowry system in Indian Marriage: Attitudes, Expectations and Practices", *International Journal of Sociology of the Family*, Vol.10, No. 1, January-June.
63. Sandhu, M.K., 1988, "A Study of Dowry Among Working and Non Working Women", *The Indian Journal of Social Work*, Vol.XLIX, No.2, April.
64. Krishnaswamy, Saroja, 1995, "Dynamics of Personal and Social Factors Influencing the Attitude of Married and Unmarried Working Women Towards Dowry", *International Journal of Sociology of the Family*, Vol. 25, No.1, Spring.
65. Nadagouda, S.G., Saroja, K., and Rao, Aruna, 1992, "Influence of Socio-Economic Factors on the Employed Hindu Woman's Attitude Towards Dowry", *The Indian Journal of Social Work*, Vol. LIII, No.4, October; Saroja, K., Chandrika, S.M., 1991, "Income and Dowry: Some Revealing Connections", *The Indian Journal of Social Work*, Vol. LII, No.2, April; Upreti, H.C. and Upreti, Nandini, 1982, "Parental Authority and Attitude of Women Students Towards Marriage and Dowry", *The Indian Journal of Social Work*, Vol. XLIII, No.3, October.

of a cultural system which is strengthened by increasing materialism where women are considered objects rather than individuals.

In fact, higher education means greater dowry. The Indian Institute of Public Opinion undertook a survey of 1,000 literates in the metropolitan cities on social customs and the incidence and impact of social change. The survey clearly reveals that better educated and higher income groups were less opposed to dowry. Education alone does not alter attitudes.[66] Paul's survey[67] of urban born, highly educated respondent of Delhi concluded that dowry was more prevalent amongst the new rich and educated sections. Education, instead of acting as a change mover, became a catalyst for dowry practices.

Hence, unless the attitude of the educated youth changes, unless the attitude of parents and family members change, unless the attitude of law enforcing agencies, police, and judges change, unless the attitude of women themselves change, dowry cannot be removed. Centuries-old practice of dowry has to be fought on a social plane by social action groups and women's organisations. Law reform and social consciousness must move together to uproot this menace. Young educated women must play a significant role in asserting their identity and putting an end to this tyrannical custom.

Women have to fight against feudal values. Inferior status and lack of self-esteem in women are the root causes of dowry. Education has not curbed dowry but is perceived as

66. —, 1978, Monthly Public Opinion Survey, 270,Vol.XXIII, No.5, March.
67. Paul, M.C., 1986, *Dowry and Position of Women in India*, New Delhi: Inter-India.

an extra qualification for marriage. The theory of economic independence has also failed as men emotionally blackmail their wives and extort money. What India needs today is a total attitudinal change. "Legal solutions alone obviously can not provide full protection to women. Ultimately, society has to come up with social safeguards by throwing up an effective system of social deterrents."[68] Social reform needs the active participation of all right thinking people.

Law, Public Opinion and Dowry

A strong force of tradition in the society results in making the codified laws mere paper transactions. In fact, any legislation will be meaningful only if society receives it in the proper spirit. In other words, only a change of attitude will make the laws more effective and the conditions of women more humane. Dowry law has gone ahead of the social values and mores.

Traditionally men have dominated the social structures and family system in India. A girl in India is brought up to be obedient, docile, patient, tolerant and self-sacrificing. They are conditioned to suffer in silence. They fear that their parents would have to suffer social ostracism. There have been incidents of young unmarried girls committing suicide to protect their parents from the burden of dowry. The first such case which caused a public outcry was that of three sisters at Kanpur, all educated, but helpless due to the dowry situation. Traditional customary laws upheld the bias against women, relegated her to purely domestic roles, conditioning them to be dependent on men. Religious customs, traditions and re-

68. Grover, Kanta, 1990, *Burning Flesh*, New Delhi: Vikas.

ligious texts have decried her social position.[69] Dowry was a compensation due to her unproductive role. Girls were treated as liability. Women's restricted access to education and employment made her dependent on men. Women in India constitute the single largest backward class facing discrimination within family and society, in work and remuneration, in options and opportunities, in power and control. Dowry is the manifestation of the inferior status of woman in society. No amount of legislation can take the place of a frontal attack on a tradition imprisoned mind which will not take its ostrich head out of the sand. Legislation which does not have popular support is doomed. A basic change of attitude must go hand in hand with legislation.[70]

Legislation cannot by itself solve deep-rooted social problems, held Nehru. The Supreme Court also observed: "The greed for dowry, and indeed the dowry system as an institution call for the severest condemnation. It is evident that legislative measures such as the Dowry Prohibition Act have not met with the success for which they were designed. Perhaps, legislation in itself cannot succeed in stamping out such an evil, and the solution must be ultimately found in the conscience and will of the social community and its active expression through legal and constitutional methods."[71]

In speaking of the Anti-Dowry and Anti-Atrocity Front, Roopa Kulkarni observes: "This front believes in dowry prohibition not only by law but by social awakening and

---

69. Gupta, Krishna, 1996, *Social Equality and The Indian Constitution*, New Delhi: S. Chand.
70. Verghese, J., 1980, *Her Gold & Her Body*, New Delhi: Vikas.
71. Supreme Court statement in the case of Shri Bhagwan Singh (1983), 2SCWR,164 at 175, 178(SC).

determined action."[72] It is unlikely that legal measures alone would be able to curb dowry. Building up of strong public opinion, and encouraging concerted action by voluntary organisations are likely to be more meaningful and effective. Women's organisations, education and mass media can play a significant role in raising awareness, mobilising public opinion against dowry.

Law Alone is Not Enough

Legislation is a partial agency of social change, in the sense that it only creates new situations or provides for change in the desired direction, but does not automatically ensure the change. Nor does it automatically create the necessary awareness, knowledge, acceptance and motivation, which are necessary prerequisites for any change. The impact of social legislation hinges upon the profound nature of change in the value systems, and attitudes and social structure prevailing in the country. Law can empower women by conferring rights on them, by strengthening the institutitonal infrastructure for enforcing such rights, and finally can cause empowerment by supporting, stimulating and monitoring the attitudinal and value changes in society.[73]

Thus legal reform and change is a bipolar process. On one hand, it creates new values and aspirations and on the other, it depends upon the willingness of the people to change. Any attempt to legislate social change without prior value change in society, amounts to the use of authority and coercive power of the state to enforce a new value frame-

72. Kulkarni, Roopa, 1983, "Anti-Dowry Front in Vidharbha," *HOW*, 6, No.3, March.
73. Sathe, S.P., 1993, *Towards Gender Justice*, Bombay: SNDT, Women's University.

work. Unless there is a measure of consensus among the generality of people about the desirability of change that law seeks to achieve, it would lead to apathy and indifference. Social legislation must be preceded by social awareness and preparedness to accept the proposed change.[74]

Law can become effective only if it is supported by social education and awakening. It is difficult to bring change by merely enacting legislations. Change goes hand in hand with educating the masses, creating awareness among the people, in fact building an enlightened and conscious public opinion. The report of the Committee on the Status of Women in India (1974),[75] held that equality of sexes as a major value could be inculcated through the educational process. Educators must bring about this much needed change in the values of the younger generation. Education would help to eliminate illiteracy, instill self-confidence among women and enhance economic opportunities by equipping them with necessary skills. Legal literacy was necessary to mobilise women and make them aware of their rights. Mass media also play an important role as opinion builders. Justice Krishna Iyer stressed the need for "social locomotion in support of social welfare legislation for women."[76] Dr. Upendra Baxi advocates reform in legal education in order to motivate the legal profession to identify themselves with the social pain and fight and demolish oppressive structures.[77] Madhu Kishwar called for social boycott of dowry, dowry wedding, and social ostracism of dowry offenders.[78] Social awareness

---

74. Sahai, Shaily, 1996, *Social Legislation and Status of Hindu Women*, Jaipur: Rawat.
75. *Towards Equality*, supra note 31.
76. *Hindustan Times*, March,13,1988.
77. *Indian Express*, March, 1989.
78. 1989, *Manushi*, 53.

must match the letter and the spirit of the law.

According to Ratna Kapur, an interactive approach to education about law must also be adopted in which women actively participate in the learning process. A feminist approach to legal literacy involves education to empower women for action and change, rather than simply conveying information about law. If women are to be empowered, equitable structures must be devised to humanise the family which includes changes in property laws to give women equal rights to inheritance.[79] Legal literacy should be provided at school and college level. Legal proceedings should be speedy and easily accessible to the people. Family courts must be set up and made functional. Police, doctors, and public prosecutors must undergo reorientation programmes. Role of the media is very significant in mobilising public opinion against social evils. Crime of "custodian suppression of evidence" must severely be dealt with. Voluntary organisations can provide support services to victimised women to pursue legal action. Dowry Prohibition Officers must serve as agents in organising legal action in collaboration with the women's organisations and in further developing the family courts as a judicial system for gender justice.

Unless the unmarried and abandoned women are given respectable status in the society, until the females are allowed to exercise control over their property and earnings and the degrading values are eliminated, the problem of dowry will persist. Any legislation will be meaningful, only if society receives it in the proper spirit. In other words, only a change of

---

79. Kapur, Ratna, "From Theory to Practice: Reflections on Legal Literacy with Women in India", in Schuler, M. and Kadirgamar-Rajasingham, S., (eds.), 1992, *Legal Literacy: A Tool for Women's Empowerment*, New York: UIIFEM.

attitude will make the laws more effective and the condition of women more humane.

A change in the attitude of legal agents, i.e., the police, public prosecutors and judges, is also essential to uproot this custom which continues to undermine Indian women. Law can bring about social change only when backed by social measures and popular support.

Social ills have to be fought on a social plane. The most effective agency to combat the inevitable consequences of the prejudice against women and negative discrimination has been the autonomous women's movement.

In 1970s, the new consciousness of women and women's issues concretised into a host of small voluntary women's group. They rallied effectively around issues of gender violence, rape, dowry deaths, *sati*, and female foeticide. They demanded law reform to check the rising tide of crime against women. For example, in the early August, 1982, 30 women's organisations in Delhi, under the banner of 'Dahej Virodhi Chetna Manch' (Anti-Dowry Consciousness Raising Forum), jointly organised a protest march against dowry. They demanded punishment and social boycott of the dowry oppressors. They were supported by general public. Women's movement was able to moblise public support and in getting Dowry Prohibition Amendment Acts enacted in 1984 and 1986. Their collective efforts actually helped in the enforcement of laws, arrest of the guilty, and conviction in some cases. The autonomous feminist groups provided support to women in distress, pressurised the courts and legislators to begin to take violence against women seriously and finally captured public attention. Dowry harassment, leading to suicides and deaths have received wide newspaper coverage and helped in arousing popular consciousness around gender violence.[80]

Despite stringent laws, atrocities, violence and crime against women continue unabated. All forms of violence against women are manifestation of unequal relationship between men and women in society. There is need for restructuring unequal social and economic relations and redefining roles of men and women. A major thrust promoting women's access to education, employment, property rights and to other resources can remove the prevailing inequalities. Women must enter into all fields of decision-making and redefine social practices and transform power structures hitherto dominated by men. A concerted and determined effort on the part of the government and non-governmental organisations to initiate changes along these lines is the need of the hour. There is need to reinforce and expedite efforts towards securing educational and economic independence of women, creating gainful employment opportunities, making cheap and purposeful legal aid available and providing secure social support and services to victims.

Women's participation in the national movement gave them equality and rights. But laws remained ineffective and unenforced till women remained passive. The politically calculated and state manoeurved moves and acts are not conducive to enhance womens right. But, the spontaneous and growing women's movement evoked a public debate on women's issues, focussed attention on structural inequalities and stressed the need for transformation of unequal relationships.

---

80. Katzenstein, M.F., 1989, "Organising Against Violence: Strategies of the Indian Women's Movement", *Pacific Affairs*, Vol. 62, No.1, Spring.

Effective change cannot be brought without a simultaneous movement to change the social and economic structures and the culture (values, ideologies and attitudes) of society.[81] Thus law can empower women only if it is preceded by public demand for change and followed by public support in favour of this change. Dowry is so deeply rooted in the Indian mindset that it cannot be removed by merely enacting laws. Social conscience has to be awakened, public opinion mobilised, and value system must be transformed so that girls would no longer be considered a liability.

81. —, 1988, *National Perspective Plan for Women*, 1989-2000, New Delhi: Government of India.

VI

Law, Public Opinion and Women

The complex interaction between law and public opinion occurs in liberal democracy and influences major policy decisions. This interplay has been examined in relation to the significant legislations affecting changing status of women in the world's two largest liberal democracies—USA and India. Whether public opinion led or followed law, was examined in the light of abortion laws in the USA and anti-dowry enactments in India.

Public Opinion Ahead of Law in USA

In mature developed democracy of the USA, public opinion is seen to lead law. The political responses of the public are registered as public opinion and it is the key variable in American politics. Page and Shapiro's study[1] concluded that

1. Page, B.I. and Shapiro, R.Y., 1992, *The Rational Public: Fifty Years of Trends in American's Policy Preferences*, Chicago: University of Chicago Press.

collective policy preferences of the American people were real, meaningful, well measured by polls, differentiated, coherent, and stable. They reacted understandably and predictably to events and new information. Public opinion was generally related to objective realities. However, political education in the US could be improved. The public deserves better education, more opportunities for participation and access to better information about public policies.

Opinions are reflection of social factors such as economic status, race and religion and these inputs were generally constant, have stabilising influences, public opinion is relatively stable.[2] Short-term fluctuations may appear, but the trend over a number of years will usually be consistent.

Research published over the last decade by Gerald Wright, Robert Erikson, and John MacIver, utilising the date from CBS News/New York Times Surveys demonstrated that aggregate ideological preferences of the citizens in the American states closely match the ideological outputs of state policy makers across a wide range of issues.[3] Robert Jackson's work (1992) also suggests that political institutions have only a slightly mediating impact on the translation of people's preferences into state policies.[4] This body of research has demonstrated the link between citizen's preferences and state

2. Monroe, Alan, D., 1975, *Public Opinion in America*, New York: Dodd, Mead and Co.
3. Erikson, R.S., Wright, G.C. and MacIver, J.P., *State House Democracy: Public Opinion and Policy in the American States*, USA: Cambridge University Press; 1987, "Public Opinion and Policy Liberalism in the American States", *American Journal of Political Science*, 31 November.
4. Robert, Jackson, 1992, "Effects of Public Opinion and Political System Characteristics on State Policy Outcome", *Publics, The Journal of Federalism*, 22 (Fall 1992).

policies. States with more liberal public tend to have more liberal policies. Citizens' preferences are generally translated into policies.

Public Opinion and the Issue of Abortion

While examining the attitude of the American people towards abortion, we found that more Americans dislike the idea of abortion, considering as a painful last resort at best, but more have come to accept the idea of permitting it under a variety of circumstances. More than 80 per cent of the population supports abortion if the woman's health is seriously endangered, if pregnancy was the result of rape and if there is a strong chance of serious defect in the baby. Only 40 per cent of the population supports abortion if the family cannot afford more children, the woman is not married and does not want to marry the man, or the woman is married and does not want any more children.[5] Thus, majority of the Americans have mixed feelings about abortion and do not want to prohibit legal abortion entirely (Scott, 1987).

In 1973, the Supreme Court ruled that the states cannot place restrictions on a woman's right to an abortion during the first three months of pregnancy. In the second trimester, the states could regulate certain of the medical aspects involved. Only during the final trimester, when medical experts generally agree that the foetus is capable of living outside the womb, can states impose restrictions on a woman's right to an abortion. The court justified a woman's decision to have an abortion on the basis of her fundamental right to privacy.

The court's decision was influenced by public opinion. In

5. "Abortion-Rights and Wrongs", *Public Opinion*, May-June, 1987: 37.

the years preceding the Roe v Wade case (1973), public opinion had become increasingly favourable to abortion (Blake, 1977; Uslaner and Weber, 1980; Johnson and Canon, 1984). In fact the opinion polls conducted by National Opinion Research Centre (NORC) in 1972 and 1973 show a dramatic increase in favourable attitudes towards legal abortion. (Ebaugh and Haney, 1980; Arney and Trescher, 1976; Tedrow and Mahoney, 1979). By 1972, public opinion moved dramatically from opposition to abortion in most cases to substantial support, if not majority support. In the decades that have followed, opinion on abortion has remained remarkably stable (Rosenburg, 1995). Polls throughout the late 1960s reported that important sub-groups of the American population were increasingly supportive of abortion law reform and repeal. Thus, public opinion mostly changed first, the Supreme Court decision in the Roe v Wade case (1973), was a consequence of opinion change (Luker, 1984; Tata-Lovich, 1988).

Majority in the US feel that abortion should not be categorically banned, but it should not be established as an absolute right. Thus, public opinion on abortion is ambivalent, wanting to keep access to abortion legal but regulating the access. Majority favour parental or spousal consent, a waiting period, and mandated counselling concerning abortion risks and alternatives.

The anti-abortion Webster case (1989) followed mild conservative drift in opinion and indications in 1982 and 1984 show that abortion opponents held their views more strongly than supporters (Scott and Schumann, 1988). Casey decision (1992) allowed the state to impose further restrictions on abortion access. In fact, organised opposition to abortion increased dramatically in the year following the court's initial decision.[6] Franklin and Kosaki (1989) hold that the Supreme Court's decision in Roe v Wade was merely recognition by the court that mass preferences on abortion were changing.

Thus, with respect to abortion, public opinion at the national level was ahead of the court. There is a general consensus that public opinion led the court's decision. Empirical research reveals that abortion policies in the states are largely responsive to public preference.[7] Where there is a greater public support for abortion in the American States, abortion policies are less restrictive.

Much of the women's movement took up the right to abortion as a key element in a broader programme of giving women more control over their lives.

Abortion: Role and Status of Women

The women's movement adopted the cause of abortion reform or repeal as a rallying point. Policies relating to reproduction has become central to the status and opportunities of women. The issue of free choice in abortion appears to involve questions of fundamental role change for women.

Policies relating to reproduction has become central to the status and opportunities of woman, for reproductive freedom provides an alternative to compulsory motherhood and family life.

Abortion debate which was originally expressed in terms of the right of privacy and medical safety is now primarily de-

---

6. Rosenburg, Gerald N., 1991, *The Hollow Hope Can Courts Bring About Social Change*, Chicago: University of Chicago Press.
7. Erikson, Robert, S., Wright, Gerald, C. and MacIver, John, P., 1993, *Statehouse Democracy: Public Opinion and Policy in the American States*, New York: Cambridge University Press.

bated in terms of a woman's right to control her own body. Feminists believe that women must have an effective choice in deciding when and if to bear a child. They feel that it is not enough to secure a legal right for abortion, but also full access to information and services from public and private agencies. They believe that women must be full participants in making decisions about their health care. This is crucial to empowerment in all social relations. Social environment has changed with the increased participation of women in the labour force. Women now aspire to other modes of self-fulfilment than motherhood. Abortion debate symbolises a much wider debate about the proper role and status of women in society: "Abortion debate is so passionate and hard fought because it is a referendum on the place and meaning of motherhood".[8] Luker holds that abortion debate is merely the tip of the iceberg of a host of concerns related to sexuality, motherhood, gender roles and family. At stake is two different definitions of the world, motherhood, the appropriate roles to men and women and the nature of morality. Pro-life activists believe that availability of abortion devalued motherhood. Abortion is seen as a threat to traditional family structure. The essence of power relationships in society may be at stake in the abortion issue. Hence, such a vigorous anti-abortion opposition sparked off in the USA.

In this era, the American public though changing in its outlook, still objected to any major changes in traditional roles of men and women. Hence, the campaign against Equal Rights Act (ERA) succeeded in shifting debate away from equal rights and focussed it on the possibility that the ERA

8. Luker, R., 1984, *Abortion and the Politics of Motherhood*, USA: University of California Press.

might bring substantial changes in women's role and behaviour.[9]

Roe justifies the state's interest in regulating abortion by adopting a purely medical definition of abortion. The court recognised an antagonistic state interest in restricting women's access to abortion on which it imposed temporal restraints. Siegel sees gender bias in foetal protection regulation. In reasoning about women's conduct to protect the unborn, state actors continue to make judgements about the duties and obligations of motherhoods. Abortion restrictive regulation is caste legislation directed against women, it plays a central role in women's subordination.[10]

Roe v Wade gave rise to paradoxical result that woman has an unrestrained right to control her body until the foetus reaches viability and then suddenly loses this right. Once she decided to carry the child to term, at that point if the well being of the potential child is at stake, she loses her autonomy, and her body may be invaded and treated for the child's sake.[11]

Daniel's study[12] has shown that during the 1980s a number of cultural, political legal, technological developments converged to bring the foetus as an independent and autono-

9. Mansbridge, Jane, 1986, *Why We Lost The ERA*, USA: Chicago University Press.
10. Siegel, Reva, 1992, "Reasoning From The Body: A Historical Perspective on Abortion Regulation and Question to Equal Protection", *Stanford Law Review*, 261, January.
11. Robertson, John, A., 1983, "Procreative Liberty and the Control of Conception, Pregnancy and Childbirth", *Virginia Law Review*, 69.
12. Daniel, Cynthia, R.,1993, *At Women's Expense: State Power and the Politics of Fetal Rights*, Massachusetts: Harvard University Press.

mous being. As the foetus gained ideological, legal and political independence from the woman, it came to be viewed as public property to be treated by a whole range of social actors, doctors, lawyers, husbands, employers and the agents of the state. Fuelled by an ideology of foetal rights, the state could now seize the pregnant woman's body as public property, restricting her access to work, jailing her for drinking or for failing to follow doctor's orders or forcing her to undergo major surgery against her will. Women's right to self sovereignty is undermined.

Public controversy over foetal rights extends beyond current legal discourse to endorse a public culture that generates more subtle forms of social control over woman. There is a crisis of reproduction, not a crisis of motherhood. It is a crisis of gender power relations. Women are demanding control over their bodies, they are refusing to conform to the dictates of gender domination, by demanding an equal place with men in the public world. This challenge to gender power relations has produced a backlash in form of attempts to enforce (or prohibit) motherhood on women.

Abortion symbolises a fundamental political struggle in the US for control and power over the ends of government. Right to life groups and anti-feminists are using politics to maintain existing power arrangements and to restore patriarchal control over women. Leaders of the reproductive rights movement are working to alter the power structure not only to achieve equality of condition for reproductive choice (Petchesky, 1984) but also to create a society in which women are released from existing social and sexual roles of homemakers, wives and mothers (Gelb and Palley, 1987). The political argument of feminists (Fried, 1990; Petchesky, 1984) is that the women's movement has to move beyond the limited goal of 'choice' to the goal of greater equality between the sexes, races and classes.[13]

In USA access to abortion is often severely restricted. While laws theoretically permit abortion on demand, in reality, women's freedom in areas such as contraception, abortion and divorce remains severely restricted. Wife's lack or limited access to outside financial resources weakens her autonomy. Unequal balance of power between the sexes leads to violence against women. In fact, violence against women in America is staggering. Incidents of wife battering, sexual assaults and rape have been constantly rising.[14] Thus, the question of abortion is entwined with the inferior status of women within the policy. In the US, power is vested in the hands of the governing elite, dominated by men. Women are generally not the decision-makers. Women were not generally included in public life, were confined to domestic spheres. Unequal gender relations tend to persist long after the social circumstances have changed. American women still make only 70 cents for every dollar men make. They are more likely to be poorer than men. They are still segregated into women's jobs and continue to be sexually harassed in the workplace. Women's movement has to go a long way to give women's equality a real meaning. Chafe has aptly commented that "the dream of equality persists—so do the obstacles to its realisation."[15] Black women and working class women in the US object to the narrowness of the abortion rights agenda. As articulated within the abortion rights movement, 'choice' simply means

---

13. Goggin, Malcolm, L., (ed.), 1993, *Understanding the New Politics of Abortion*, New Delhi: Sage.
14. Becker, Mary, Bowman, C.G. and Torrey, M., 1993, *Feminist Jurisprudence Taking Women Seriously: Cases and Materials*, American Case Book Series, Minnesota: West Publishing Co.
15. Chafe, W.H., 1989, *The Paradox of Change, American Women in the Twentieth Century*, New York: Oxford University Press.

the choice to have an abortion or not. In the absence of access to abortion services, decent health care, decent child care, acceptable life options for their children, 'choice' is a hollow and abstract concept far remote from the concrete realities experienced by women of colour (Petchesky, 1984).

Abortion in India

The experience of Indian women in the area of reproductive rights and policies is different from their American counterparts. 'Choice' is not a central component or platform of the Indian women's movement. For, abortion is available on demand for family planning purposes.[16] Western feminism has traditionally taken the position that the right to abortion is a fundamental and non-negotiable demand.[17] In the USA, the feminist discourse on abortion is generally conducted in the language of liberal rights. In developing countries like India, abortion is seen as a population control policy, often aggressively promoted by the government for economic development. Abortion is rather a socially mandated consequence of the economic imperatives of the state. In fact, the progressive attitude of the Indian state to abortion is dictated by compulsions other than a commitment to women's liberation.[18] In India, unlike in the USA, the issue of abortion has not been subject to many debates because it was part of the

16. Patel, Vibhuti, 1989, "Sex Determination and Sex Pre-Selection Tests in India: Modern Techniques for Femicide", *Bulletin of Concerned Asian Scholars*, 21:2-10.
17. Luker, Kristin, 1984, *Abortion and the Politics of Motherhood*, Berkeley: University of California Press.
18. Menon, Nivedita, 1993, "Abortion and the Law: Questions for Feminism", *Canadian Journal of Women and the Law*, Vol.6. No.1.

government's family planning and population control measures.

The word 'abortion' remains abhorrent to Indian culture and mindset, it is considered equivalent to murder. Therefore, word 'abortion' was substituted with the words termination of pregnancy. The Medical Termination of Pregnancy Act (MTPA) was passed in 1971, which legalised abortion under specific conditions such as danger to the health of the mother and/or the child. Section 3 of the Act facilitates a pregnant woman to terminate her pregnancy voluntarily (if she is a minor or lunatic, written consent of the guardian is necessary) by a registered medical practitioner if the length of pregnancy is of twelve weeks. In case the length of pregnancy is between twelve and twenty weeks, then the concurring opinion of two medical registered practitioners is needed. An abortion is permitted if the doctor certifies that the continuing of the pregnancy would endanger the life of the pregnant woman or would affect her physical or mental health seriously or there is substantial risk of the child being born with physical or mental abnormalities or handicaps. The Act allows MTP facility not only to protect the mental health of the raped victim but also to a woman whose pregnancy is the outcome of the failure of a contraceptive device. Further, a woman can seek an abortion on the ground of her "actual or reasonably foreseeable environment" being not conducive to her pregnancy.

Thus, the MTP Act of 1971 laid down liberal grounds through which women obtained the right to safe, scientific and legal abortions. MTPA has been hailed as a landmark social legislation, which confers on women the right of privacy and freedom of choice. It would put a stop to illegal and unsafe abortions performed by non-qualified, untrained, and ill-equipped medical practitioners under unhealthy conditions.

The Act has been termed as a milestone in the modernisation of Indian society through the instrumentality of law. It has a direct impact on population control and in achieving economic and social development and would play a role in the emancipation of women from the age-old fear of abortion being considered as a sinful and criminal act.[19] But critics hold that liberalising abortion in a country like India, where woman have little say in most matters, and where there is no strong health education programs and where abortion is seen as a family planning measure, it cannot be seen as promoting women's right but as aggravating hazards to women's lives.[20] The Act is not so much concerned about women's health and autonomy, but treats abortion as a crime unless performed under specified conditions. These conditions confer a monopoly on medical opinion which has the power to decide whether the woman meets the requirements of the Act.

Further, a civil right to abortion does not amount to a social right carrying all the necessary enabling conditions that make a concretely realisable and universally available. A really safe abortion is possible only by embedding abortion services in the full range of social services—health care, prenatal care, child care, safe and reliable contraception, sex education etc.[21] Legislation has not been buttressed by safe and humane abortion services.[22] Abortion when used as a

---

19. Gaur, K.D., 1995, "Abortion and the Law in Countries of Indian Subcontinent, Asian Region, United Kingdom, Ireland and the U.S.A.", *Journal of the Indian Law Institute*, Vol.37, No.3, July-September.
20. Karakal, Malini, 1991, "Abortion Laws and the Abortion Situation in India", *Issues in Reproductive and Genetic Engineering*, Vol.4, No.3.
21. Jesani, Amar and Iyer, Aditi, 1993, "Women and Abortion", *EPW*, Vol. XXVIII, No. 48, November 27.
22. Ibid.

method of family planning is bound to become a tool in the hands of the demographers and doctors, politicians and administrators to control the reproductive autonomy of women. It is bound to have a coercive impact on women.

The debate about the reproductive freedom and women's choice has taken a new ominous turn in India with the growing practice of selective abortion of female foetuses after sex determination tests during pregnancy. Amniocentesis was originally resorted to as a technique to determine genetic abnormalities in the foetus at the prenatal stage and suggestive abortion on diagnosing such abnormalities. Knowledge about the sex of the foetus was an additional information obtained from the test, but the result was that most of the couples who discovered that the foetus was female, selected abortion. Social pressures within the family lead many women in India to opt for female foeticide. Subsequently, through an order of the Indian Council of Medical Research, the use of amniocentesis test was restricted to suspected cases of genetic diseases. Between 1977 and 1987 three circulars to government departments at the centre and in the states made the use of prenatal sex determination for the purpose of abortion a penal offence.

The ban on the use of this technology in government institutions had led to its privatisation and commercialisation. Sex determination clinics mushroomed all over the country. Unscrupulous doctors used the technology to mint easy money. Districts, which lack such basic amenities as clean drinking water and electricity have prenatal sex determination clinics. This reveals the wide popularity of these tests and the misogynist orientation of the Indian society.

Sex determination techniques are increasingly being used in India for selective extermination of female foetuses. This phenomenon is known as foeticide.

The Times of India, a prominent newspaper, reported that between 1978 and 1983 in Bombay, 78,000 female foetuses were aborted after the tests. In 1986-87, 30,000 to 50,000 female foetuses were apprehended to have been aborted. Between 1982 and 1987, the number of clinics for sex determination multiplied manifold—in the city of Bombay alone, it increased from 40 to 248. The practice continues undaunted.

The Registrar General of India has admitted to abortion of 3.6 lakh female foetuses in India in 1993-94, an estimate based on hospital births alone.[23] The most disturbing evidence was presented in a study conducted by a subcommittee of the Federation of Obstetricians and Gynecologists Societies of India. Out of 8,000 cases, the study reported that 7,999 were aborted when the test results showed a female foetus[24] (Ravindra, 1986; *The Statesman*, 17 December, 1984). Another survey was done by Professor R.P. Ravindra of the Pharmacy College of the SNDT University of Bombay. In his research on 1,000 cases in Bombay, he could not find a single case of a male foetus being aborted, whereas 97 per cent of the foetuses identified as female were aborted (Ravindra, 1986:9).

Finally, another set of comprehensive results was produced by Sanjeev Kulkarni of the Foundation for Research in Community Health. For his report, titled *Sex Determination Tests and Female Foeticide in Greater Bombay*, he interviewed

---

23. Arora, Dolly, 1996, "The Victimising Discourse Sex Determination Technologies and Policy", *EPW*, Vol. XXXI, No.7, February 17.
24. Ravindra, R.P., 1986, "The Scarcer Half", Bombay: Centre for Education and Documentation; 1987, "Struggle Against Sex Determination Techniques: Unifinished Battle", *EPW*, 21 March.

fifty gynecologists; 84 per cent of them admitted that they were performing sex determination tests. It was estimated that about 50,000 sex-selective abortions were taking place annually in Bombay by 1987. There were 250 clinics in Bombay alone and 600 in the whole state of Maharashtra (*Health Monitor*, 1988).[25]

A private clinic in Bombay had performed 15,914 abortions in 1984-85, all of which took place after the results of amniocentesis tests.[26] Like dowry, the preference for sons has extended beyond the Hindu community, and sex diagnosis tests are now being requested by Muslim and Sikh families as well. There were similar reports from other states about increases in abortions after tests results were known.

Parents have argued that it is less expensive for them to abort the female foetus than to bear the expenses of rearing a child and paying for a dowry. Thus, discrimination against women in India begins even before she is born.

A campaign against the practice of prenatal sex determination was launched by women's groups as well as civil liberties and health movements. In October, 1984, a broad coalition, the Forum Against Sex Determination and Sex Preselection (FASDSP) was set up to carry on a sustained campaign against sex determination. The Forum has used a combination of public moral persuasion and education, and legislative changes to bring about its objective of stopping the abuse of sex determination tests. The campaign gained momentum and the issue received wide media publicity and sympathy and popular support.

---

25. Manju, Parikh,1990, "Sex-Selective Abortions in India: Parental Choice or Sexist Discrimination?" *Feminist Issue*, Vol. 10, No.2.
26. Vanaik, A., 1986, "Female Foeticide in India: Sex Determination Leads the Way", *The Times of India*, Bombay, 20 June.

The FASDSP seeks to end not just the selective abortion of female foetuses, but sex pre-selection tests as well. It calls for a ban on such pre-selection—techniques and for the regulation of the introduction of all new technologies in future. The Forum activists campaigned to mobilise the health authorities against the misuse of these technologies.

These tests pose a serious threat to the demographic balance, have exposed women to additional risks, and reinforce gender bias. Female foeticide has resulted in adverse sex ratio and declining female population in India. The sex ratio has been declining steadily during the past decades, down from 946 females per 1,000 males in 1951 to 929 per 1,000 males in 1991. In some states of northern India it has fallen to 600 women to 1,000 man (*The Times of India*, New Delhi, June 19, 2000). Advanced technology in prenatal care which should have worked to empower woman has ironically become an instrument to eliminate the girl child before birth. In India, being born a female itself is treated as a deformity. The sex determination tests were widely used with the specific intention of abortion female foetus.[27] They have devalued women, reduced her role to that of carrier of male progeny. These tests are being widely used by commercial and professional interests for profit making by exploiting the prevailing social prejudice against woman. Women's dependent status leaves little room for autonomous decision making by her. Women who choose to abort the female foetuses are generally influenced by the prevailing social pressures or compelled to act by husbands or families and are not really exercising their free will. Sometimes, the practice of selective

---

27. Agnes, Flavia, 1992, "Protecting Women against Violence: Review of a Decade of Legislations, 1980-1989", *EPW*, Vol. XXVII, No. 17, April 25.

abortion of female foetuses is justified as a form of population control.[28]

Thus, the crucial point is that abortion must be available to women who want it while selective abortion of female foetuses must be stopped. There is need for banning the misuse and at the same time for regulating the proper use of these techniques.[29] In 1988, the Government of Maharshtra enacted the Maharashtra Regulation of the Use of Prenatal Diagnostic Techniques Act which prohibited prenatal sex tests outright, with dire penalties for law-breakers. But, in practice, the law is blatantly ignored and abortion of female foetuses continue unabated. In 1994 Indian Parliament outlawed sex determination again, with similarly stiff penalties, not only against doctors, but also against their women patients if it can be proved that they were not under family pressure. This is simply victimising the victims, as women in India hardly have any choice.

A major cause for the alarming increase of foeticide and adverse sex ratio is the tradition of the dowry. A daughter is normally an unmitigated expense, someone who will never contribute to the family income and who upon marriage, will take away a considerable part of the family's fortune as her dowry. In the recent decades, the tradition of dowry has become more oppressive and has assumed the form of continuous demand of the bride-takers causing untold strain to the bride-givers. Modernisation and free market consum-

---

28. Kulkarni, Sanjeev, 1986, "Sex Determination Tests and Female Foeticide in the city of Bombay", report commissioned by the Secretary to the Government, Department of Health and Family Welfare, Government of Maharashtra.
29. Ravindra, R.P., 1990, "Campaign Against Sex Determination Tests", *Lokayan Bulletin*, 8.3:27-42.

erism have perpetuated dowry especially amongst the educated classes. Market price of the highly placed bridegroom has shown enormous hike. Harassment and torture of the bride for extorting more money and consumer goods resulting sometimes in bride burning or suicides continue on a large scale despite relatively stringent provisions. When dowry murders occurred, witnesses were not forthcoming, evidence was destroyed, and neighbors did not wish to intervene. Violence within the home constitutes a private affair, goes largely unnoticed or is generally hushed up. The culprits are rarely arrested and even more rarely convicted. Dowry is essentially responsible for the continuing cultural devaluation of Indian women. The dowry system is at its strongest among Hindu communities, although it is now widely practised by other groups. It is among Hindus that son preference finds strongest favour. While a daughter is considered a liability, a son is glorified as he remains with the family, continues the family name, looks after his parents in their old age and performs the necessary rituals for salvation after their death. A daughter would marry and leave the parental home and is thus treated as '*parayadhan*' or stranger's wealth, to be nurtured and trained and given away at the expense of a suitable dowry. The strong son preference and undesirability of a daughter stemmed from this situation and remained deeply entrenched in the Indian psyche and gave rise to the new form of eliminating baby girls through selective abortion of female foetuses. Couples were attracted by sensational advertisements such as "Better Rs. 500 now (for sex determination test) than Rs. 50,000 later for a daughter's wedding". Female foeticide is the most extreme form of discrimination against girls.

The conditions which perpetuate gender inequality need

to be changed with a sense of urgency. Need for state intervention through appropriate legislation is necessary. However legislation is embedded in the dominant values of a system. It often fails to deliver justice to women who are systematically exposed to the exploitative mechanisms of patriarchic structures.[30] Law fails to deliver justice resulting from its sexist interpretation by biased functionaries. There is an urgent need to prevent the misuse of amniocentesis technique for sex determination. There is a need for restructuring the social attitudes through public education and consciousness raising. It is essential to mobilise public opinion for protection and care of the girl child. It is necessary to ameliorate the causes of son preference and female devaluation in Indian society. We must fight for incentives for educating daughters for increase in women's employment, opportunities for women's land and inheritance rights and for women's political empowerment.

The critical issues in the Indian context include access to safe abortions and safe child birth facilities, as well as general health care, nutrition, rather than the legal right to abortion.

Feminist activists strongly advocate far reaching structural changes that would make 'choice' more authentic. It is the extreme sexism and patriarchy in society that leads women to make the choice to abort the female foetus, therefore it is not a 'free' choice. Therefore, rights over one's bodies are not natural but constituted as legitimate only

30. Arora, Dolly, 1996, "The Victimising Discourse: Sex Determination Technologies and Policy", *EPW*, Vol, XXXI, No.7, February 17; Menon, N., "Rights, Law and Feminist Politics: Rethinking Our Practice", in Mukhopadhyaya, S., (ed.), 1988, *In the Name of Justice*, New Delhi: Institute of Social Studies Trust, Manohar.

within specific discursive political practices (Menon, 1992, 1995). Woman's choice in the Indian context must certainly take into account the misuse of sex determination and the monstrous proportion of female foeticide causing a demographic imbalance in the country. More than legislative intervention, there is need for mobilising public opinion and changing the social outlook through public education.

In USA, research done on sex preference has shown that majority of men and women prefer sons, especially prefer first borns to be sons (Steinbecker and Holmes, 1987). However, the use of selective abortion based on sex is rare in the USA. They recommend that every effort be made to stop further research on sex determination technologies, and to persuade people, especially women, not to use such technologies.

Law Ahead of Public Opinion in India

In India, the Constitution promises complete equality to women and gave her equal rights. The founding fathers hoped to build up an egalitarian democratic polity and a liberal society. They tried to use law for the massive task of social engineering in order to reform the old order based on gross caste, gender and class inequalities. A number of social legislations enacted in the post-independence era sought to revolutionise the position of women in India. But social attitudes and thinking remained deep-rooted in antiquated and irrational customs, traditions, and prejudices. As long as the basic perceptions of the society and the law-enforcing agencies remained anti-women gender justice cannot be promoted by paper enactments. This was the experience of the legislators who tried to be more progressive in social matters, and move ahead of the prevailing public opinion. Their enthusiasm soon turned into pessimism they had to slow down their speed, make compromises, often diluting the spirit of the statutes or pass token and weak legislation. Conservative social values hampered the proper enforcement of these laws reducing them to mere paper statutes without any transformative capacity.

Anti-Women Orientation of the Indian Society

Indian society is based on caste hierarchy and patriarchy, both of which have marginalised large sections of population on the basis of caste and gender. Caste constitutes an all-embracing form of social organisation where the status of the individual is determined by birth and is inherited. Caste system begun by the principles of endogamy and traditional occupation, became over burdened with considerations of purity and pollution and gradually became rigid and inflexible. It tended to create a feeling of superiority and inferiority, fostered narrow caste loyalties, bred social inequalities and was particularly harsh towards the lower castes and women.

Women and Caste

Caste operated in a complex manner degrading women to an inferior status, creating in her servile mentality and in shaping social attitudes, behaviour patterns and ideological values justifying her subordinate position. Caste exerted tight constraints on women. This control involved two major aspects. One was women's disinheritance from immovable property in the form of land, and their exclusion from the productive economy involving removal from public life to the domestic sphere. The second was the far greater control exercised by men over women's sexuality, imparted through the new law books known as the *Smritis*. These advocated strict monogamy for women and marriage before puberty for girls. She was not to study the Vedas or perform any sacrifices and knowledge of *Shastras* was forbidden for her. A woman was grouped with the Sudras and along with them was called '*papayoni*', i.e., of sinful birth or one preordained to a low station in life.[31]

Inter-caste marriages were socially condemned as it led to '*varnasamkara*' (Manu X,12). Another manifestation of caste inequality was the differential status of bride 'giver' and 'taker', the latter always considered as superior. The bride givers had to give compensation in form of dowry. There was an inbuilt inequality in Hindu arranged marriage, where the bride's side was only supposed to give but never take anything in return. Especially, in the upper castes, women were confined to domestic work, their physical mobility restricted by caste norms. Birth of a daughter was a source of anxiety as her marriage would impose tremendous financial strain on the family. Widow remarriage was shunned. By the early medieval period, she was expected to follow her dead husband to the funeral pyre and to become a '*sati*'.[32] Caste extolled the self sacrificing and self effacing image of women through the ritual practices, emphasised the dominant role of her as a faithful wife and devoted mother and obedient daughter. The caste system provided strong partilineal social structure along with features like the giving away of the girls in marriage, importance of the son for continuity of the line, authority and superiority of the male, significance of virginity etc., which

31. 1974, *Towards Equality: Report of the Committee on the Status of Women in India*, New Delhi: Government of India.
32. Kane, P.V., 1941, *History of Dharma Shastras*, Vol.II, Part I, Pune: Bhandarkar Oriental Research Institute.

provided ideological legitimation for subordination of women. With the advent of the Aryans, the patriarchal social system became firmly rooted and women were subordinated to men. Patriarchy glorified the ideology of male superiority and female subservience. It saw woman primarily as an instrument of sex and procreation (preferably of males) and as a piece of husband's property. Marriage remained central to a woman's life and through marriage a man acquired property rights over his wife. For she was given in marriage to her husband to fulfil her productive and reproductive role. Women were withdrawn from public life, secluded in homes, denied education and assigned chiefly child bearing and child rearing functions.

Patriarchal Family Structure

Fundamentally in all Hindu families, whether joint or otherwise, man is seen as the head of the household, as the 'karta', the doer, the bread earner and woman is seen as dependent on him and is treated primarily as an instrument of male sexual enjoyment and reproduction of children. Motherhood is glorified and the pressure to produce sons is enormous as they continue the family line and are expected to support their aged parents, while daughters by contrast are treated as liabilities in a patriarchal society. Men control women's reproductive power, her labour, her sexuality, and her mobility. Male dominance is thus rooted in the gender division of labour. Men continue to work in the public sphere; such work generally involves earning money. Women's work often remains restricted to domestic sphere (Mukhopadhyay and Seymour, 1994; Kishwar, 1991; Liddle and Joshi, 1986; Standing, 1991; Der'ne, 1994). This accounts for continuing decline in women's participation in the paid labour force (Calman, 1992; CSWI, 1974).

Woman has little control over the economic resources and is reduced to economic dependence as man's ward or property. Their primary responsibilities were child rearing and nurturing the young, the old and the ill. Women had to do all the household work, which is generally unrecognised and unpaid. In modern times, working woman shoulder a double burden of working outside the home and also doing all the housework. Particularly in northern India, women by and large do not have independent property rights.

Hindu society breeds sex inequality and maintains an anti-female bias at all levels, in both open and latent ways. From cradle to the grave, females are subjected to numerous acts of prejudice, denial and discrimination, oppression and violence within the family, at the place of work and in society.[33] Girls are socialised from their childhood to be dependent on males. She is denied an independent identity. Her existence is always described in relation to the man. Hindu women was conditioned to believe that marriage is her destiny and her only hope to salvation was complete devotion and service to her husband. She was and still continues to be taught to become a dutiful wife and worship her husband, no matter how cruel, unfaithful or immoral he might be. '*Pativrata*' ideology as preached by the ancient law givers idealised the docile, patient and virtuous wife, completely devoted to her husband, absolutely submissive and sacrificing and never complaining. Laws of Manu insist that, "a husband must be constantly worshipped as a God by a faithful wife" (Manu, V, 154). Women needed to be strictly disciplined in order to curb her inherently 'evil' and 'weak' character. Thus the theory of the perpetual tutelage of woman was clearly

---

33. Chandrashekhar, S., 1994, *India's Abortion Experience, 1972-1992*, USA: University of North Texas Press.

formulated (*Yajnavalkya Smriti*, 1.77).[34] India's patriarchal family system places women at the mercy of men who exercise unlimited power over them and often use violence as a tool to control them. Violence is legitimised power structures within the family and has the sanction of society. The Indian state too is patriarchal and continues to leave the household based authorities the control over the lives of their women. Inspite of a number of face saving laws, dowry based violence or female foeticide are carried on with impunity within the household.[35]

Mukhopadhyaya and Seymour (1994) conclude that patrilocal family structure and ideology in India emphasise the importance of family and the centrality of men within families, restrict women to the private sphere, give men greater authority over women, exert family control of marriage arrangements and women's sexuality. Family honour is upheld as important and is closely connected with women's modesty. Hindu gender ideology emphasises modesty, obedience, self-sacrifice, and attachment to the home.[36] Hindu social system was thus built on the value system which regards women as inferior and servile. It conditioned her to accept a secondary role, remain dependent, suffer in silence, and never revolt against an oppressive family environment.

Such retrogressive social attitudes and opinions have come in the way of enactment and enforcement of social leg-

---

34. Gupta, Krishna, 1995, *Social Equality and the Indian Constitution*, New Delhi: S.Chand & Co.
35. Nirmala, Bannerjee, 1998, "Whatever Happened to the Dreams of Modernity? The Nehruvian Era and Women's Position", *EPW*, Vol, XXXIII, No.17, April 25.
36. Mukhopadhyaya, Carol and Susan Seymour, (eds.), 1993, *Women, Education and Family Structure in India*, Boulder: C.O. Westview.

islations striving for social transformation.

When public opinion was not very supportive of progressive legislation, Nehru had a difficult time in getting the Hindu Code Bill enacted. The code aimed at reform of the Shastric Hindu law, and evoked strong protest from the orthodox sections headed by the then President of India, Dr. Rajendra Prasad. The consideration of the Hindu Code Bill was successfully stalled. The original bill had to be broken into four separate parts to facilitate their enactment five years later. The original bill was diluted resulting in a set of legislations which was more symbolic rather than substantial in character.[37] The opposition from the die-hards was so strong that some of the basic inequalities rooted in the joint family system and the personal inheritance laws could not be removed. Mitakshara coparcenary giving preferential rights to sons in the joint family property was retained. In addition to this, the unrestricted freedom of testation which is used to disinherit women heirs continues even today to be a part of the Hindu Laws of Succession. Besides these, there is a restriction imposed on the right of the daughter to demand partition of the dwelling house. Thus, in the 1950s, public policy had to adjust itself accordingly for fear of not being able to enforce the law.

Similarly, is case of dowry, the Dowry Prohibition Act which was passed in 1961 proved ineffective and the menace of dowry assumed frightening proportions. The Act had made both asking and giving of dowry a legal offence to be punished by imposition of fines. Gifts were allowed. The offence was non-cognisable and bailable and the Act similarly

37. Som, Reba, 1994, "Jawaharlal Nehru and the Hindu Code: A Victory of Symbol Over Substance", Great Britain: Modern Asian Studies, 28, 1 February.

failed to achieve its purpose. The ineffectiveness of the Act manifested at different levels. First, there were hardly any case filed under the Act and there were less than half a dozen convictions in the period between the enactment and the amendment. So the purpose of the Act as a deterrent factor was totally lost.

Thus, anti-dowry legislations could not check the ever increasing atrocities against women on account of insufficient dowry cases being brought up. For almost two decades, while the dowry menace kept spreading along with violence, little was done. It needed a Dahej Virodhi Chetna Manch (DVCM)—a coordinating forum of women's groups and organisations through its various forms of struggle like street corner meetings, neighbourhood demonstrations, dharnas, public marches to draw the attention of the government and to make it finally act (Lotika Sarkar, 1995).

Such collective efforts could no longer be ignored and the government responded by referring the Dowry Amendment Bill to the Joint Parliamentary Committee. Based on its recommendations, the Act was amended first in 1984 and again in 1986. Activists thus mobilised public support in changing the law.

The Joint Parliamentary Committee, in its report, strongly asserted that the best precursor of such social reforms was in social thinking behaviour and the creation of strong public opinion. Laws could prove effective only if they were backed by major sections of the society. Wide gulf or gap between the social climate and the laws of the land results in frictions which are not good for the health of the community. Law can no doubt be used as instruments for engineering social welfare. There is, however, a limit up to which laws can be ahead of community's thinking and social climate. If laws move too much ahead, they would have to cry halt or retrace their steps. If they remain static, they will fail to keep pace with the march of time. Although interaction between law and social progress is inevitable, it is also essential to keep in view the need of harmony between social thinking and legal processes. The committee felt that law could be effective if two conditions were satisfied: first, supportive public opinion must accompany the law, secondly, administrative willingness to implement that law. With the help of the media and social support, the women's movement was able to focus the attention of the people on the most pressing social problem. Their efforts widened awareness of the changed manifestation of dowry and its linkages with socio-economic and structural issues. These attempts created legal and political space for the women's movement (Govind Kelkar, 1984).

It is necessary to enact pragmatic laws and to make their enforcement effective by creating public opinion in their favour. However, stark social realities cannot be changed by merely enacting social legislatives. Centuries of thinking cannot be altered by legal measures. Thus, in India, law tried to lead public opinion but did not prove very effective. Only when anti-dowry legislation is supported by social awakening, it yields positive results.

Women's economic dependency, lack of equal inheritance rights, the familial ideology which naturalises and universalises the construction of women as dependent, dutiful, self sacrificing wives and mothers, all perpetuate the low status of women in society. Dowry is simply an offshoot of the unequal social system which has conditioned women to accept an inferior role and suffer in silence. The DVCM memorandum (1982) clearly holds that dowry was a widespread social phenomenon and was "linked with the entire gamut of inferior female conditioning". "Its increasing incidence is symptomatic of the continuing erosion of women's status and devaluation of female life in independent India."

In India, as we have seen, law was ahead of public opinion but remained ineffective, unenforced. Only when public opinion was mobilised by the women's movement in the 1970s and 1980s against dowry, it resulted in change of public policy and better enforcement of the same.

Despite innumerable social legislations enacted in their favour, women continue to be victims of exploitation, discrimination and violence at home and outside. Deep-rooted ideas about male superiority enable men to freely exercise unlimited power over women's lives. Legislation often reflects the dominant values of the system. Often laws were callously framed more as a token gesture than due to any genuine concern in changing the status quo of women.[38]

Social change must be preceded by transformation of value structure. There was a great ambivalence towards equality as is clear in discussions and debates on women's rights in the 1930s, 1940s and 1950s (Everettt, 1979; CSWI Report, 1974). The Constituent Assembly Debates reveal that framers were eager to grant equality in political and legal spheres but not in the spheres of marriage and the family. Women were granted abstract fundamental rights but when it came to radically altering the iniquitous family and social frameworks, the framers fell back on Directive Principles, which had no legal sanctions behind them.[39]

---

38. Agnes, Flavia, "Violence Against Women: Review of Recent Enactments", in Mukhopadhyaya, S., (ed.), 1998, *In the Name of Justice*, New Delhi: Manohar.
39. Gupta, Krishna, supra note 34.

Tradition, caste, custom and familial ideology have all restrained women from realising equal rights and freedom. Discriminatory and biased attitudes and prejudices are holding them back and reinforcing their subordination. The ultimate power to bring about change rests with the people. Only any enlightened and conscious public opinion can act as a catalyst of change through law.

Law and Women in Liberal Democracies

Both USA and India have liberal democratic systems. Formal equality has been granted to women in both the countries. Indian Constitution grants equal rights to women, but personal laws in marriage, divorce, inheritance take precedence, and perpetuate gender inequality in the family and society. Women in the US still do not have equal rights under the constitution, although there are several provisions for equal pay at the federal levels. Women's formal economic rights do not spell equality in the workplace. The Equal Rights Act passed by the US Congress in 1972 could not be ratified by three-fourths of the states. In both the countries, the wage gap and sex segregation of occupations are outcomes of patriarchal, capitalist social organisation. Despite the passage of the Equal Pay Act in 1963 and Title VII of the Civil Rights Act in 1964, there is still a reluctance on the part of some persons to alter ingrained habits of thought and behaviour and accept the changing gender roles in principle. For historically, women as group were viewed as psychologically and socially different from men. Therefore, they were not to be included in public life. They were generally confined to domestic work. Customs are deep rooted and do not alter immediately with the passage of laws. The unequal gender relationships have a tendency to persists long after the social circumstances have changed. Women are still concentrated in the largely segregated traditionally female occupations which usually involve domestic skills. Notwithstanding the legislation concerning equal rights, men in personnel and decision making positions have found ways to circumvent the law.

Laws that make divorce difficult, abortions illegal and that prescribe restrictive rules in employment are subtle reminders that a woman's role is that of a domestic help and child producer within the confines of marriage.

Liberal democratic states tend to be patriarchal ones in part because of the historical traditions and in part because power structure are based on race, class and gender. Such state encode the idea of family as a separate location in law and practice (Eisenstein, 1984; Mackinnon, 1983). The state itself is male with respect to its methods and objectives: "the liberal state coercively and authoritatively constitutes the social order in the interests of men as a gender through its legitimating norms, forms, relation to society, and substantive politics" (Mackinnon, 1989). In the past, women were socialised to accept the social role of nurturant in a male dominated home. These unequal relationships have a tendency to persist long after the social circumstances have changed. Patriarchy refers to the systematic arrangement of social, economic and political power in ways that benefit male members of society and ensure the subordinate status of women.

In USA, the second wave feminist movement focussed on how women's oppression within the private sphere of the family was the root of women's subordination. The state through its insistence on the preservation of the traditional family structure at all costs, places the wife in a position of dependence on her husband. Her lack or limited access to outside financial resources weakens her autonomy. Unequal balance of power between the sexes leads to violence against women.[40]

Women in India constitute the single largest backward class facing discrimination within the family and society, in work and remuneration, in options and opportunities, in power and control. They constitute a great mass of illiterate and powerless humanity. Roots of gender inequality go deep both in time and in people's psyche and are deeply embedded in the Indian social structure based on caste hierarchy and patriarchy.

Indian women remain at best second-class citizens. In 1974, the Committee on the Status of Women in India (CSWI) produced a significant document highlighting women's declining status, role and participation. The report revealed that majority of women in India did not enjoy the rights and opportunities guaranteed to them by the Constitution and were generally ignorant of their legal rights. The socio-cultural settings restricted their role in the family's decision making process and in society generally. Steady marginalisation of women in the labour force had taken place and large majority remained unrepresented politically. Thus, women suffered from inequality of class (economic situation), status (social position) and political power. They remained a minority continuously exposed to injustice.[41]

---

40. The amount of violence against women in America is staggering: one out of every two married women will be beaten on at least one occasion by her husband; One out of every three girls will be sexually assaulted before age 18; and almost one out of every two women is raped or survives an attempted rape. [Becker, M., Bowman, G.G., Torrey, M.,(ed.), 1994, *Feminist Jurisprudence, Taking Women Seriously*, USA: West Publishing Co.].
41. 1974, *Towards Equality: Report of the Committee on the Status of Women in India*, New Delhi: Government of India.

The National Perspective Plan 1988-2000 clearly admits that the development policies have failed to give justice to women. Laws, education, health and family planning and communication all reveal a sexist bias. The plan acknowledges the necessity to give women more space and create an egalitarian social structures.

Discrimination against woman starts even before she is born. The rising use of amniocentesis to determine the sex of the unborn child has led to widespread female foeticide. It is within the family that she is nurtured to an inferior status and her role is devalued. It is here that she is deprived of her rightful share of food, care and education and silenced into resignation and passive acceptance of a dependent status. Incidence of violence and crime against women have risen. India's National Crime Records Bureau has recorded an increase of 40 per cent cases of sexual harassment, 15.2 per cent in dowry deaths, 87.2 per cent in the smuggling of girls in 1998 over 1997. Dowry is based on the cultural ethos which views brides as objects to be passed from one social group to another. It diminishes the social power of the brides and endangers her life.[42] Dowry deaths have risen by over ten times in the last 15 years. From 427 cases of bride burning in 1983 the number has gone upto 6,917 in 1998 (NIP, June 15, 2000). Dowry system is extremely demeaning to a woman and symbolises her inferior status and complete insignificance. Media continue to project negative images of women—as marketable objects, as powerless commodities or parasitical consumers. Consumer culture and perverse advertising has generated widespread anti-women values in the

42. Chhabra, Sagari, 1986, *Dowry Death in India: A Double Bind Perspective* (A Thesis for M.A. in Communication), Washington State University Department of Communication.

male-dominated world. Majority of women are prevented from making headway economically because of lesser social mobility, limited access to job opportunities, confinement to low paid and less skilled jobs, in the unorganised sector. Women's presence in the workforce is just 19 per cent. Near total disinheritance from the means of production, land and technology has perpetuated her growing marginalisation in the economy. It is common in most parts of country for women, both rural and urban, to forgo their rights in parental property. They have been driven to the backwaters of politics. Beyond the periodic exercise of their voting rights, women are extremely limited in the electoral politics or in the decision making process. They have never emerged as a potential voter's bloc and are generally under represented in the legislatures. There are only 12 per cent women representatives in the Rajya Sabha and 7 per cent in the Lok Sabha and 3.8 per cent in the government, of this only 3.2 per cent are at ministerial level. Globalisation has increased illicit trade in drugs, women and weapons and contributed to rising violence and crime against women in South Asia and free market economy has led to the commodification of the female body.[43] Nearly 61 per cent women are illiterate (1991 census) and are largely unaware of the laws made in their favour. Women's rights therefore remain on paper, unimplemented, unenforced, and ineffective. The effect of personal laws is the subordination of women in all spheres that they cover—property rights, rights within the family, maintenance rights, divorce rights, guardianship and adoption rights.

Implementation of progressive laws, passed to ensure equality, is hampered by caste and patriarchal family struc-

---

43. Giri, Mohini, "The Peaceful Force", *The Hindu*, June 11, 2000.

ture. Traditional values have often resulted in the negative role played by the enforcement machinery. Legal machinery can play only a limited role in the liberation of women, it cannot do away with the gender injustice, embedded in the unequal structures of the society. Social order must be redefined, power structures hitherto dominated by men must be transformed.

Struggle for gender justice became a global movement in the 20th century. Gender justice includes environmental justice, economic justice and social justice. It is this indivisible concept of justice that will guide the struggle of women's movements in the present times.[44] In the movements for social transformation, gender relations was a key component along with other objectives of human rights, environment and the end of unjust social orders.[45] Women's social positions have been significantly affected by processes of change and development, expansion of education, legal reforms and their own movements. Women have, through consciousness raising movements, struggle for equal rights, self-determination, democracy and justice made their growing presence felt in the public sphere. Their growing participation in the labour market has created a social and cultural revolution. Drive for women's rights has taken on a powerful global momentum as we enter the 21st century.

However, cultural backlash is occurring in some parts in the form of 'fundamentalist movements' for the veiling of

---

44. Shiva, Vandana, 1995, "Gender Justice and Global Apartheid", *Mainstream*, Vol., XXXIII, No.44, September, 23.
45. Agnihotri, Indu and Mazumdar, Vina, 1995, "Changing Terms of Political Discourse: Women's Movement in India, 1970s-1990s", *EPW*, Vol. XXX, No.29.

women or the abolition of abortion. Globalisation has accentuated traffic in women and girl for sexual exploitation and has brought women under the hegemony of the global capital made them economically vulnerable and has led to feminisation of poverty. Women constitute the majority of the world's poor. They are generally confined to 'unproductive work' and segregated into low paid jobs. Sex discrimination and sexual harassment have limited their incomes and economic mobility.

The Platform for Action (PFA) adopted at the Beijing Conference (September, 1995) aimed at removing gender inequalities. It focussed on twelve specific areas of concern like poverty, education, health, violence, armed conflicts, economic disparity, power sharing, institutions, human rights, mass media, environment and the girl child. The PFA had been hailed as the culmination of women's struggle for justice and equal opportunities in their diverse contexts around the world. The 23rd special session of the UN General Assembly was held during June 5-9, 2000, to review the implementation of the PFA. However, the reports presented by the nations establish that justice still eludes women. Canada which tops the ranking among all nations in the Human Development Index is credited by the Canadian NGO report with a situation where its women continue to experience severe disadvantages and restructuring of social programmes have worsened their economic condition, single mothers and unattached women are poor.

In USA, despite the current unprecedented period of economic growth, too many women and children continue to live in poverty, particularly the rural women. More women work for low pay in insecure jobs. Women in the former socialist countries of Europe were suffering from negative impact of privatisation and destabilising influence of the economy in transition. The African report claimed that Africa was worse off in terms of armed conflicts, rendering women more vulnerable to violence, HIV and AIDS.[46]

India's situation is quite dismal. There has been no improvement in women's participation in parliament (9 per cent according to statistics released by Inter-Parliamentary Union), crime against women has gone up drastically, there has been an alarming decline in the sex ratio and discrimination against female is astounding. According to the Human Development Report, 2000, released by the UN, India is ranked 128th in the human development index. India needs to spend more on human development, on primary health and education and do away with human inequalities. However, the report has lauded India's efforts for significant progress in participation of women in local politics, creative use of public interest litigation, effectiveness of its vibrant civil society, and mobilisation of its democratic institution (*Hindustan Times*, 30 June, 2000).

Discrimination and exploitation on the basis of gender continues to be a global phenomenon. Women's access to education, health, employment and political sphere remain restricted. Poverty, class, caste and religious fundamentalism are factors that impinge on women, adding to the discrimination arising out of gender. Women's battle against inequity and disparity continues.

Thus law secured formal rights for women in liberal societies. The liberal discourse precludes an understanding or inequity into the deeper relationships of oppression underlying and sustained by the law.

---

46. Mythili, Sivaraman, "Justice Still Eludes Women", *The Hindu*, June 21, 2000.

Law Must Follow Public Opinion

Law generally follows public opinion in liberal democracies. Public opinion consisting of social customs and norms, habits and practices, social sentiments and beliefs, prejudices and biases based on the collective experience of the people, evolves over the ages and tends to remain stable. Change in public opinion is generally slow and gradual. Majority opinion also tends to be conservative and is not generally supportive of radical changes.

In liberal democracies people get an opportunity to participate at the time of elections, elect the policy makers, freely express their views through the mass media, present their demands, influence the decision making. Legislators, or the people's representative cannot afford to ignore the public opinion. In such participative and representative democracy, law and opinion are closely interrelated and interdependent. Generally, law follows public opinion as is seen in the USA. This was clearly established in the abortion issue. Only when public opinion became increasingly supportive of women's right to choice that the Supreme Court legalised abortion nationwide in Roe v Wade case in 1973. Majority of the Americans support abortion in certain difficult situations and do not support either the pro-choice or pro-life extremes. Abortion attitudes in the US has remained more or less stable. The empirical studies have documented that the court's decision reflected change in public opinion—they did not legislate change.

However, India's experience constitutes a remarkable contrast to this trend of law following opinion. When law attempted to march ahead of public opinion as in India, it did not prove very effective.

In India, some progressive policy makers like Nehru and

Ambedkar were keen to use law as an instrument of social transformation and change. Their attempts at constitutional engineering to bring about a radical change in the status of women, encountered tremendous resistance from the conservative sections representing the predominant social opinion of that time. There ensued a long debate between the progressive section led by Prime Minister Nehru who were determined to modernise the traditional society and the conservative school headed by the President Dr. Rajendra Prasad. The old guards felt that the Hindu Code Bill was an attempt to destroy the Hindu society and was alien to Hindu tradition and culture. They were not prepared for a fundamental change in the status of women in the family and at home. The President held that the Prime Minister had not properly consulted the people and the proposed code had completely ignored the public opinion. The feeble voice of the few women members remained unheard. Rallying against the die-hards, the Law Minister Dr. B.R. Ambedkar resigned out of sheer despair, while Nehru agreed to substantial dilution of the original code in order to placate the patriarchal social values. What was enacted as Hindu Code Bill merely granted formal rights to women and substantial equality in the family and property, at home and at work. Thus social legislation, finally enacted after prolonged debate and controversy, remained restricted and weakly enforced. In fact, traditional attitudes grounded in the concept of inherent inferiority of women have hampered the egalitarian ethos proclaimed in the constitution.

Dowry Prohibition Acts too could not override the entrenched social values of the patriarchal family system and the caste stratified social system in India. Dowry continues to enjoy the status of the ancient custom and is justified for ensuring a daughter's security. The Act of 1961 tried to confine dowry to reasonable limits and did not ban it altogether. Dowry continues in the form of gift giving and pervades the Indian psyche and culture and is very common even amongst the educated sections of society. The conservative social climate has encouraged the negative role played by the enforcement machinery and contributed to the ineffectiveness of the law and growing violence against women. Dowry prohibition laws were not very effective as the social opinion was not opposed to dowry and social norms and values justified the girl's dependent status and glorified the culture of silence and sacrifice.

India's experience establishes that law without the support of public opinion remains a dead letter, ineffective and unenforced. Any attempt to legislate social change without prior value change in society is bound to prove futile. India has learnt that law can act as an instrument of social engineering provided it is supported by public opinion. Change in law should be pre-conditioned by change in the attitudes of the people.

It is necessary to articulate public opinion and mobilise it in favour of social legislation. This can be done through education and social movement.

Awareness of law must be created in the people through education, media, legal literacy at all levels of society and a strong and favourable public opinion must be created in favour of social legislation for its effective implementation. In India, dowry has to be fought not by law alone but on a social plane by generating a social and cultural revolution through consciousness raising. Autonomous women's movement was successful in bringing about law reform, amendments better implementation of laws, and played an effective role in generating and mobilising public awareness about the menace of dowry. Anti-dowry movement led by DVCM was to a large extent able to mobilise social opinion against dowry and constituted a step forward in transformation of policy and society. Law must be preceded by social awakening and a change in values.

The comparative analysis of the American and Indian policy making establishes the close congruence between opinion and law. Generally, public opinion inspires and generates making of public policies as is seen in the USA. But, in case of India, law tried to lead the change in public opinion but encountered very strong public resistance and had to be modified in the line of the prevailing social opinion. This clearly establishes that public opinion must lead enactment of public policies if they are to be effective in liberal democracies. Law can become an effective instrument of change if led as well as followed by public opinion.

Bibliography

Achar, M.R., and T. Venkanna, 1993, *Dowry Prohibition Act and Rules (Central and States): With State Amendments*, 3rd revised ed. by B.K. Sharma, Allahabad: Law Book Co.

Agarwal, Bina, (ed.), 1989, *Structures of Patriarchy: The State, The Community and The Household*, London: Zed Books.

Agarwal, Bina, 1994, *A Field of One's Own: Gender and Land Rights in South Asia*, Cambridge: Cambridge University Press.

Agarwal, Bina, 1988, "Who Sows? Who Reaps? Women and Land Rights in India', *Journal of Peasant Studies*, Vol. 15, No. 4.

—, (ed.), 1988, *Structures of Patriarchy: State, Community and Household in Modernizing Asia*, New Delhi: Kali for Women.

Agnihotri, Indu, and Mazumdar, Vina, "Changing Terms of Political Discourse: Women's Movement in India, 1970s-1990s", *EPW*, Vol. XXX, No.29, July,29.

Ahuja, Ram, 1987, *Crime Against Women*, Jaipur: Rawat.

Allen, C.K., 1987, *Law in the Making*, 7th ed., First Indian Reprit, 1997, New Delhi: Universal Law Publishing Co.

Allport, F.H., 1937, *Toward a Science of Public Opinion*, *Public Opinion Quarterly*. 1(1), 7-23.

Almond, G.A., and Verba, S., 1963, *The Civic Culture: Political Attitudes and Democracy in Five Nations*, Princeton: Princeton University Press.

Altekar, A.S., 1956, *The Position of Women in Hindu Civilization*, Banaras: Motilal Banarsidass.

Anthony, M.J., 1985, *Women's Rights*, New Delhi: Dialogue.

Aristotle, 1952, *Politics*, R.M. Hutchins (ed.), 1952, *Great Books of the Western World*, Vol. 9, Chicago: Encyclopedia Britannica.

Arney, William Ray, and Trescher, William, H., 1976, "Trends in Attitudes Towards Abortion, 1972-1975", *Family Planning Perspectives*, Vol.8, No.3, May-June.

Arora, Dolly, 1996, "The Victimizing Discourse: Sex Determination Technologies and Policy", *EPW*, Vol. XXXI, No.7, February, 17.

Austin, John, 1832, *The Province of Jurisprudence Determined.*

—, 1863, *Lectures on Jurisprudence*, (ed.), 2.Vols., London: Murray.

Austin Granville, 1999, *Working a Democratic Constitution*, New Delhi: Oxford University Press.

Awasthi, S.K., and Lal, U.S., 1986, *Dowry Prohibition*, Allahabad: National Law Agency.

Baig, Tara Ali, 1976, *India's Women Power*, New Delhi: S.Chand.

Baker, Ross, K., Epstein, L.K., and Forth, R.D., 1981, "Matters of Life and Death: Social, Political and Religious Correlates of Attitudes about Abortion", *American Politics Quarterly*, Vol. 9, No.1, January, 1981, pp.89-102.

Banerjee, Nirmala, 1989, "Working Women in Colonial Bengal: Modernisation and Marginalisation", Sangari, Kumkum, and Vaid, Sudesh, (eds.), *Recasting Women: Essays in Indian Colonial History*, Delhi: Kali for Women.

Banerjee, Nirmala, (n.d.), *Interaction between Cultural Patterns, Development Forces and Women's Position*, CWDS Paper.

Bannerjee, Nirmala, 1998, "Whatever Happened to the Dreams of Modernity? The Nehruvian Era and Women's Position", *EPW*, Vol. XXXIII, No.17, April, 25.

Bardhan, Kalpana, 1986, "Women: Work, Welfare and Status. Forces of Tradition and Change in India", *South Asia Bulletin*, Spring, pp.3-16.

Barnartt, Sharon, N. and Harris, Richard J., 1982, "Recent Changes in Predictors of Abortion Attitudes", *Sociology and Social Research*, Vol. 66, April, pp.320-34.

Basu, Rumki, 1985, "Dowry and Right to Property", *Mainstream*, 13 April.

Baxi, Upendra, 1985, "Taking Suffering Seriously: Social Action Litigation in the Supreme Court of India," in Gandhi, P.K.(ed.), *Social Action Through Law*, New Delhi: Concept.

—,1986, *Towards a Sociology of Indian Law*, New Delh: Satvahan.

Becker, Mary, Bowman, Cynthia Grant, Torrey, Morrison, 1994, *Feminist Jurisprudence Taking Women Seriously, Cases and Materials,* American Case Book Series, USA: West Publishing Co.

Bennett, W.L., 1980, *Public Opinion in American Politics*, New York: Harcourt Brace & Jovanovich.

Berger, A.A., 1989, *Political Cultural and Public Opinion*, New Brunswick, NJ: Transaction Publishers.

Blake, Judith and J. H., del Pinal, 1980, "Predicting Polar Attitudes toward Abortion in the United States", *Abortion, Parley*, (ed.) Burtchaell, J.T., Kansas City, KS: Andrews and McMeel.

Blake, Judith, 1971, "Abortion and Public Opinion: The 1960-1970 Decade", *Science* 171, 12:540-49.

Boserup, E., 1970, *Women's Role in Economic Development*, New York: St. Martin's Press.

Bryce, J., 1909, *The American Commonwealth*, 3rd ed., 2 Vols., London and New York: Macmillan.

Buhler, G., 1886, *The Laws of Manu:* (Translated with Extracts from Seven Commentaries), London: Oxford.

Buutap, Nguyenphuc, 1979, *Legislation, Public Opinion and the Press: An Interrelationship Reflected in the New York Times' Reporting of the Abortion Issue*: Thesis (Ph.D), Chicago: University of Chicago.

Callahan, Daniel, 1979, "Abortion and Government Policy", *Family Planning Perspectives*, Vol. II, No.5, September-October.

Caplan, L., 1984, "Bridegroom Price in Urban India: Class, Caste and Dowry Evil among Christians in Madras", *MAN*, 19, 2, 216, 233.

Carmines, E.G., and Stimson, J.A., 1989, *Issue Evolution: Race and the Transformation of American Politics,* Princeton: Princeton University Press.

Carroll, Lucy, 1978, "Colonial Perceptions of Indian Society and the Emergence of Castes' Association", *Journal of Asian Studies*, 37, pp. 233-50.

—, 1987, "Dowry Prohibition Legislation: Some Suggestions for Change". *Journal of the Indian Law Institute*, Vol. 29, No. 1, [January-March], pp.48-59.

—, 1989, "Law, Custom and Statutory Social Reform: The Hindu Widow's Remarriage Act of 1856", J. Krishnamurty, (ed.), *Women in Colonial India*, New Delhi: Oxford University Press.

—, 1991, "Daughter's Right of Inheritance in India: A Perspective on the Problem of Dowry", *Modern Asian Studies*, 25, 4, pp.791-809.

CBS/New York Times Surveys, 1989-1991.

Census of India, 1991, series 1: "India: Provisional Population Totals," Paper I of 1991, New Delhi: Registrar General and Census Commissioner.

Chafe, W.H., 1989, *The Paradox of Change American Women in the Twentieth Century*, New York: Oxford University Press.

Chakravarthy, Gargi, 1984, "Dowry: Can Law Alone Fight the Feudal Outlook?", *Mainstream*, 12 May.

Chakravarty, Uma, 1989, "Whatever Happened to the Vedic Dasi? Orientalism, Nationalism and a Script for the Past", Sangari K., and Vaid, S., (eds.), *Recasting Women: Essays in Colonial History*, New Delhi: Kali for Women.

Chandra, Bipan, 1999, *India After Independence*, India: Viking, Penguin India.

Chandran, Geeta, 1986, "Daughter in Distress", *Mainstream*, 25 (14), 20 December, pp.32-3.

Chatterjee, B., Singh, S. S., and Yadav, D.R., 1971, *Impact of Social Legislation on Social Change,* Calcutta: The Minerva Associates.

Chatterjee, Partha, 1990, "The Nationalist Resolution of the Women's Question", Sangari, Kumkum, and Vaid, Sudesh, (eds.), *Recasting Women: Essays in Indian Colonial History*, New Delhi: Kali for Women.

Chatterjee, Shoma A., 1988, *The Indian Women's Search for an Identity*, New Delhi: Vikas.

Chattopadhya, Kamaladevi, 1983, *Indian Women's Battle for Freedom*, New Delhi: Abhinav.

—, 1939, *The Awakening of Indian Women*, Calcutta: Government of India Publication.

Chauhan, Richa, 1995, *Dowry in Twentieth Century India: A Window to the Conflict of Caste, Class and Gender*, A Dissertation in Sociology, Stony Brook: State University of New York.

Coleman, J., 1988, *Markets, Morals and the Law*, Cambridge: Cambridge University Press.

Combs, M.W., and Welch, S., 1982, "Blacks, Whites and Attitudes Towards Abortion", *Public Opinion Quarterly* 46:518-20.

Constitutional Assembly Debates, 1949, New Delhi: Government of India.

—, Vol. II, 20.1.1947 to 25.1.1947.

—, Vol. III, 28.4.1947 to 2.5.1947.

—, Vol. IV, 14.7.1947 to 31.7.1947.

—, Vol. VII, 4.11.1948 to 8.1.1949.

Cook, Elizabeth Adell, Jelen, Ted G., Wilcox, Clyde, 1992, *Between Two Absolutes: Public Opinion and The Politics of Abortion*, USA: Westview Press.

Cook, Elizabeth Adell, Jelen, Ted G., and Wilcox, Clyde, 1992, *Choice vs. Life: Public Attitudes Toward Legal Abortion*, USA: Westview Press.

Coole, Diana, 1988, *Women in Political Theory From Ancient Misogyny to Contemporary Feminism*, Sussex: Wheatsheaf Books.

Corbett, M., 1991, *American Public Opinion: Trends, Processes, and Patterns*, New York: Longman.

Craig, Barbara Kinkson, and O'Brien, David M., 1993, *Abortion and American Politics*, New Jersey: Chatham House Publishers.

Davis, James. F., Foster, Jr. Henry, H., Jeffery, C.R., Davis, E.E., 1962, *Society and the Law*, USA: The Free Press of Glencoe.

Davis, James, Alen, and Smith, Tom W., 1996, The General Social Survey: 1972-1996, Cumulative Codebook, Chicago: National Opinion Research Centre, University of Chicago.

Daynes, Byron, W., and Tataloyich, Raymond, 1984, "Religious Influence and Congressional Voting on Abortion", *Journal for the Scientific Study of Religion* 23:197-200.

—, 1992, "Presidential Politics and Abortion", 1972-1988. *Presidential Studies Quarterly* 22:545-61.

de Beauvoir, Simone, 1971, The Second Sex, (trans and ed.), Parshley, H.M., New York: Alfred Knopf.

de Souza, Alfred, (ed.), 1975, *Women in Contemporary India*, New Delhi: Manohar.

Derrett, J.D.M., 1957, *Religion, Law and the State in India*, London: Faber and Faber.

—, 1984, "What the Dharmasastra Has to Say about Dowry", Lariviere, Richard (ed.), *Studies of Dharmasastra,* Calcutta: KLM.

Desai, Neera, (ed.), 1988, *A Decade of Women's Movement in India*, Bombay: Himalaya Publication.

Desai, A.R., 1985, "Women's Movement in India", *Economic and Political Weekly*, Vol.XX, No. 23, 8 June.

Desai, Neera, and Patel, Vibhuti, 1985, *Indian Women: Change and Challenge in the International Decade, 1975-1985*, Bombay: Popular.

Desai, Neera and Krishnaraj, Maithreyi, 1987, *Women and Society in India*, New Delhi: Ajanta.

Desai, Neera, 1982, "Emergence and Development of Women's Organizations' (mimeo), Research Unit on Women's Studies, Bombay: SNDT University,

Deshpande, V.S., 1984, *Women and the New Laws*, Chandigarh: Chandigarh Publications Bureau, Punjab University.

Devendra, Kiran, 1985, *Status and Position of Women in India*, New Delhi: Shakti Books.

Devendra, Kiran, 1994, *Changing Status of Women in India*, New Delhi: Vikas.

Dhagamwar, Vasudha, 1974, *Law, Power and Justice: Protection of Personal Rights under the IPC*, Bombay: N.M.Tripathi.

Dhar, Lalita, 1988, "Dowry Legislation in India: Retrospects and Prospects", *Indian Socio-Legal Journal,* Vol. 14, Nos. 1-2, pp.129-141.

Dhruvrajan, Vanaja, 1981, *Hindu Women and Power of Ideology,* Massachusets: Bergin and Harvey.

Dicey, A.V., 1905, *Law and Public Opinion in England During the Nineteenth Century*, UK: Macmillan.

—, 1996, *First Indian Reprint*, New Delhi: Universal Book Traders.

Diwan, Paras, 1985, "The Dowry Prohibition Law", *Journal of the Indian Law Institute,* Vol. 27, No. 4, pp. 564-571.

—, 1987, *Dowry and Protection to Married Women*, New Delhi: Deep and Deep.

—, 1994, *Women and Legal Protection*, New Delhi: Deep and Deep.

—, 1995, *Dowry and Protection to Married Women*, 3rd ed., New Delhi: Deep and Deep.

—, 1997, *Law Relating to Dowry, Dowry Deaths, Bride-Burning, Rape and Related Offences*, New Delhi: Universal Law Pub. Co.

Dowrkin, R., 1986, *Law's Empire*, London: Fontana.

—, 1994, *Life's Dominion: An Argument About Abortion, Euthanasia and Individual Freedom*, New York: Vintage Books.

Dowry Prohibition Act, 1961.

Dowry Prohibition (Amendment) Act, 1982.

Dowry Prohibition (Amendment) Act, 1986.

Dreze, Jean, and Sen, Amartya, 1995, *India: Economic Development and Social Opportunity*, New Delhi: Oxford University Press.

Eisenstein, Zillah, R., (ed.), 1979, *Captalist Patriarchy and the Case for Socialist Feminism*, New York: Monthly Review Press.

—, 1984, *Feminism and Sexual Equality: Crisis in Liberal America*, New York: Monthly Review Press.

—, 1988, *The Female Body and the Law*, Berkeley: University of California Press.Engels, F., 1977, *The Origin of Family, Private Property and State*, Moscow: Progressive Publishers.

Erikson, R.S., McIver, J.P., and Wright, G.C., Jr., 1987, "State Political Culture and Public Opinion", *American Political Science Review* 81, 797-813.

Erikson, R.S., Wright, G.C., Jr., and McIver, J.P., 1989, "Political Parties, Public Opinion, and State Policy in the United States", *American Political Science Review* 83, 729-749.Everett, Jana Matson, 1979, *Women and Social Change in India*, New Delhi: Heritage.Feldman, Stanley, 1988, "Structure and Consistency in Public Opinion: The Role of Core Beliefs and Values", *American Journal of Political Science* 32:416-40.

Friedan, Betty, 1963, *The Feminist Mystique*, New York: V.Gollancz.

Friedmann, W., 1972, *Law in a Changing Society*, London: Stevens and Sons.

Frug, Mary Joe, 1992, *Postmodern Feminism*, New York: Routledge.

Gallup, G., and Rae, S.F., 1940, *The Pulse of Democracy: The Public-opinion Poll and How it Works*, New York: Simon & Schuster.

Gallup, G., 1966, "Polls and the Political Process: Past, Present and Future", *Public Opinion Quarterly*, 29, 544-549.

—, 1972, *The Sophisticated Poll Watcher's Guide*, Ephrata, PA: Science Press.

—, 1989, "Attitudes on Abortion Little Changed since Supreme

Court's 1973 Ruling", Gallup Report No. 281:16-23.

Gamson, W.A., 1988, "A Constructionist Approach to Mass Media and Public Opinion", *Symbolic Interaction* 11, 161-174.

Gandhi, M.K., 1919-1932, *Young India*, Ahmedabad.

—, (ed.), *Harijan – A Journal of Applied Gandhism*, 1933-1955 in 19 Vols., New York and London: Garland Pub. Inc.

—, 1958, *Women and Social Injustice*, Ahmedabad: Navajivan Publishing House.

Gandhi, Nandita, and Shah, Nandita, 1991, *The Issues of Stake: Theory and Practice in the Contemporary Women's Movement in India*. New Delhi: Kali for Women.

Gandhi, P.K., 1985, *Social Action Through Law*, New Delhi: Concept.

Gangrade, K.D., 1978, *Social Legislation in India*, Vol. I, New Delhi: Concept.

Ghadially, Rehana, (ed.), 1988, *Women in Indian Society: A Reader*, New Delhi: Sage.

Ghadially, Rehana and Kumar, Pramod, 1988, "Bride-burning: The Psycho-social Dynamics of Dowry Deaths", Ghadially, R., (ed.), *Women in Indian Society: A Reader*, New Delhi: Sage.

Ghose, S.K., 1984, *Women in a Changing Society*, New Delhi: Ashish.

—, 1989, *Indian Women through the Ages*, New Delhi: Ashish.

Gilligan, C., 1982, *In a Different Voice*, USA: Harvard University Press.

Ginsbers, B., 1986, *The Captive Public: How Mass Opinion Promotes State Power*, New York: Basic Books.

Ginsberg, Faye D., 1989, *Contested Lives: The Abortion Debate in an American Community*, Berkeley: University of California Press.

Glasser, Theodore L., and Salmon, Charles, T., 1995, *Public Opinion and the Communication of Consent*, USA: The Guilford Press.

Glasser, T.L., 1991, "Communication and the Cultivation of Citizenship", *Communication*, 12, 235-248.

Goggin M.L., ed., 1993, *Understanding the New Politics of Abortion*, New Delhi: Sage.

Gonslaves, Lina, 1993, *Women and Law*, New Delhi: Lancer.

Goody, Jack, R. and Tambiah Stanley, J., (eds.), 1973, *Bridewealth and Dowry*, Cambridge: Cambridge University Press.

Granberg, Donald, Granberg, B.W., 1980, "Abortion Attitude 1965-1980: Trends and Determinants", *Family Planning Perspectives*, Vol. 12, No. 5.

—, 1985, "Social Bases of Support and Opposition to Legalized Abortion", Sachdev, Paul, (ed.), *Perspectives on Abortion*, London: Sacrecrow Press.

Grover, Kanta, 1990, *Burning Flesh*, New Delhi: Vikas.

Gupta, Krishna, 1996, *Social Equality and the Indian Constitution*, New Delhi: S.Chand.

Habermas, J., 1989, *The Structural Transformation of the Public Sphere: An Inquiry into a Category of Bourgeois Society*, Cambridge, Massachusetts: MIT Press.

Hacker, P.M.S. and Raz. J., 1977, (eds.), *Law, Morality and Society*, Oxford: Clarendon Press.

Hadley, Janet, 1996, *Abortion Between Freedom and Necessity*, UK: Virago Press.

Haider, Saraswati, 1999, "National Policy for Women in India 1996: A Critique", *Social Scientist*, Vol.25, Nos. 3-4, March-April.

Haksar, Nandita, and Singh, Anju, 1986, *Demystification of Law for Women*, New Delhi: Lancers Press.

Haksar, Nandita, 1985, "Women and Public Interest Litigation: A Decade of Struggle", *Samya Shakti*, Vol. 2, No.1, CWDS, New Delhi.

Herbst, S., 1993, *Numbered Voices: How Opinion Polling has Shaped American Politics*, Chicago: University of Chicago Press.

Hooja, S.L., 1969, *Dowry System in India: A Case Study*, New Delhi: Asia Press.

Inglehart, R., 1990, *Culture Shift in Advanced Industrial Society*, Princeton: Princeton University Press.

Jain, Devaki, (ed.), 1975, *Indian Women*, New Delhi: Government of India Publications.

—, (ed.), 1980, *Women's Quest For Power: Five Case Studies*, New Delhi: Vikas.

Jain, Ranjana, S., 1992, *Family Violence in India*, New Delhi: Radiant.

Jeffrey, Patricia, 1979, *Frogs in a Well: Indian Women in Purdah*, New Delhi: Vikas.

Jesani, Amar, and Iyer, Aditi, 1993, "Women and Abortion", EPW, Vol. XXVIII, No. 48, November, 27.

Jethmalani, Rani, 1995, (ed.), *Kali's Yug, Empowerment, Law and Dowry Deaths*, New Delhi: WARLAW, Har-Anand Pub.

Jethmalani, Rani, and Dey, P.K., 1995, "Dowry Deaths and Access to Jusitce", Jethmalani, R., (ed.), Ibid., pp.36-78.

Joseph, Ammu, and Sharma, Kalpana, (eds.), 1994, *Whose News? The Media and Women's Issues*, New Delhi: Sage.

Kane, P.V., 1941, *History of Dharmashastra*, Vol. II, Part I, Poona: Bhandarkar Oriental Research Institute.

Kapur, Promilla, 1974, *The Changing Status of the Working Women in India*, Bombay: Vikas.

Kapur, Ratna, Cossman, Brenda, 1996, *Subversive Sites: Feminist Engagements with Law in India*, New Delhi: Sage.

Kapur, Ratna, (ed.), 1996, *Feminist Terrain in Legal Domains: Interdisciplinary Essays on Women and Law in India*, New Delhi: Kali for Women.

Katzenstein, M.F., 1989, "Organising against Violence Strategies of the Indian Women's Movement", *Pacific Affairs*, Vol. 62, No. 1, Spring.

Kaur, Amrit, 1948, *To Women*, Ahmedabad: Navajivan Pub. House.

Kaushik, Susheela, (ed.), 1985, *Women Oppression: Patterns and Perspectives*, New Delhi: Shakti Books.

Keer, Dhananjay, 1964, *Mahatma Jotirao Phooley: A Father of Indian Social Revolution*, Bombay: Popular Prakashan.

Kelkar, G., 1984, "Women's Movement Studies: A Critique of the Historiography", *Samya Shakti*, Vol. 1, No. 2.

—, 1985, "Women and Structural Violence in India", Occasional Paper, No. 4, New Delhi: CWDS.

—, 1985a, "Violence against Women: An Understanding of Responsibility for their Lives", *Samya Shakti*, Vol. 2, No. 1.

—, 1992, *Violence Against Women. Perspectives and Strategies in India*, New Delhi and Shimla: Manohar, and Indian Institute of Advanced Study.

Khan, M.Z., and Ray, R., 1984, "Dowry Death", *Indian Journal of Social Work*, pp. 303-315, Vol. XLV No. 3.

Kishwar, Madhu, 1984, (ed.), *In Search of Answers: Indian Women's Voices from Manushi*, London, Zed Books.

—, 1986, "Dowry: To Ensure Her Happiness or to Disinherit Her", *Manushi*, No.34., pp. 2-13.

—, 1988, "Rethinking Dowry Boycott", *Manushi*, No. 48; pp.10-13.

—, 1988a, "The Struggle of the Indian Women", *Philosophy and Social Action*, Vol. 14, No. 4,

—, 1989, "Dowry and Inheritance Rights", *Economic and Political Weekly*, Vol. XXIV, No. 11, 18 March.

—, 1989a, "Inheritance, Not Dowry is the Issue", *The Sunday Observer*, 1 January, p.15.

—, 1989b, "Deprived of Dignity", *Legal News and Views*, 3 (4), April, pp.7-8.

—, 1989c, "Dwory Deaths: The Real Murders", *Indian Express Magazine*, April, pp.1, 6.

—, 1989d, "Towards More Just Norms for Marriage: Continuing the Dowry Debate", *Manushi*, No. 53, pp.2-9..

—, 1989e, "Continuing the Dowry Debate", *The Economic and Political Weekly*, Vol. XXIV, No. 49, 9 December.

—, 1990, "Inheritance Rights for Women", *Manushi*, No. 57.

—, 1993, "Dowry Calculations: Daughter's Rights in her Parental Family". *Manushi*, No.78, pp. 8-17.

Kosambi, Meera, 1994, *Women's Oppression in the Public Gaze*, (ed.), Bombay: SNDT Women's University.

Krishnamurthy, J, (ed.), 1989, *Women in Colonial India*, New Delhi: Oxford University Press.

Krishnamurthy, S., 1981, *The Dowry Problem: A Legal and Social Perspective*, Bangalore: IBH Prakashan

Krishnaraj, Maithreyi, (ed.), 1986, *Women's Studies in India: Some Perspectives*, Bombay: Popular Prakashan.

—, 1988, "Relevance of Research on Women", *Economic and Political Weekly,* 16 January.

Krishnaswamy, Saroja, 1995, "Dynamics of Personal and Social Factors Influencing the Attitude of Married and Unmarried Working Women Towards Dowry", *International Journal of Sociology and the Family,* Vol. 25, No.1.

Kumar, Radha, 1989, "The Women's Movement", *Seminar,* 355, March.

—, 1993, (ed.), *The History of Doing: An Illustrated Account of Movements for Women's Rights and Feminism in India, 1800-1990*. New Delhi: Kali for Women.

Kumari, Ranjana, 1989, *Brides are Not for Burning: Dowry Victims in India*, New Delhi: Radiant.

Law Commission of India, 1975, *Sixty Fourth Report on the Suppression of Immoral Traffic in Women and Girls Act, 1956*, New Delhi: Government of India.

Law Commission of India, 1976, *Sixty Sixth Report On the Married Women's Property Act of 1874,* New Delhi: Government of India.

Law Commission of India, 1979, *Eighty-First Report on Hindu Widows Remarriage Act of 1856,* New Delhi: Government of India.

Law Commission of India, 1983, *Ninetieth Report on the Grounds of Divorce Among Christians in India: Section 10 of the India Divorce Act, 1869*, New Delhi: Government of India.

Lee, P.R., and LeRoy, L.B., 1985, "Abortion, Politics and Public Policy", Sachdev, Paul, (ed.), *Perspectives on Abortion*, New Jersey: The Sacrecrow Press.

Leftwich, Adrian, (ed.), 1990, *New Developments in Political Science: An International Review of Achievements and Prospects*, England: Edward Elgar Pub.

Liddle, Joanna and Joshi, Rama, 1985, *Daughters of Independence, Gender, Caste and Class in India*, London: Zed Books.

Lok Sabha Debates, 1954, Vol. V, Part II, pp7253-4.

Lok Sabha Debates, (IXth Session), 1959, Vol. 36, No. 14 (3 Dec.1959), New Delhi.

Lowell, A.L., 1913, *Public Opinion and Popular Government*, New York: Longman, Green and Co.

Luker, Kristin, 1984, *Abortion and the Politics of Motherhood*, USA: University of California Press.

Luthra, A., 1983, "Dowry Among the Urban Poor: Perception and Practice", *Social Action*, Vol. 33 No. 2., pp. 207-220.

Mackinnon, C.A., 1987, *Feminism Unmodified, Discourses on Life and Law*, Cambridge, Massachusetts: Harvard University Press.

MacKinnon, C.,1989, *Toward a Feminist Theory of the State*, Cambridge, Massachusetts: Harvard University Press.

Mansbridge, Jane, 1986, *Why We Lost the ERA?*, Chicago: University of Chicago Press.

Mathew, Anna, 1987, "Attitudes Towards Dowry", *The Indian Journal of Social Work*, Vol. XLVIII No. 1, pp.95-102.

—, 1990, "Dowry and its Various Dimensions" in Devasia, L. and Devasia, V.V., (eds.), *Women in India*, New Delhi: Indian Social Institute, pp. 79-88.

Mazumdar, Vina, 1976, "The Social Reform Movement in India-From Ranade to Nehru", Nanda, B.R., (ed.), 1976, *Indian Women From Pardah to Modernity*, New Delhi: Vikas.

—, 1979, *Symbols of Power: Studies of Political Status of Women in India*, Bombay: Allied.

—, 1985, "Emergence of Women's Question and Role of Women's Studies", New Delhi: CWDS.

Menon, Nivedita, 1993, "Abortion and the Law: Questions for Feminists", *Canadian Journal of Women and the Law,* Vol 6.

Menski, Werner, 1997, "The Dowry Problem: Can Legal Remedies Work?". *London: Law Review,* Issue 10, Antumn/Winter, pp. 129-132.

—, 1997b, "The Dowry Problem: Progress in Legal Remedies". 1997 (2) *Kerala Law Times,* Journal section, pp. 67-75.

—, 1998, (ed.), *South Asia and the Dowry Problem*, New Delhi: Vistaar.

Mies, Maria, 1980, *Indian Women and Patriarchy*, New Delhi: Concept.

Mill, J.S., 1952, *Considerations on Representative Government*, Hutchins, R.M., (ed.), *Great Books of the Western World,* Vol. 43, Chicago: Encyclopedia Britannica. (Original work published in 1861)

Mischler, William, and Sheehan, R.S., 1993, "The Supreme Court as a Counter Majoritarian Institution: The Impact of Public Opinion on Supreme Court", *American Political Science Review*, Vol. 87, No.1, March.

Monroe, A.D., 1975, *Public Opinion in America*, New York: Dodd, Mead and Co.

Monthly Public Opinion Survey, 1978, 270, Vol. XXIII, No. 5, March.

Mukhopadhyaya, Swapna, 1993, (eds.), *In the Name of Justice: Women and Law in Society*, New Delhi: Manohar.

Nadagonda, S.G., Saroja, K., and Rao, Aruna, 1992, "Influence Socio-Economic Factors on the Employed Hindu Women's Attitude Towards Dowry", *The Indian Journal of Social Work,* Vol. LIII, No.4, October.

Nair, Janaki, 1996, *Women and Law in Colonial India: A Social History*, New Delhi: Kali for Women.

Nanda, B.R., 1976, (ed.), *Indian Women from Pardah to Modernity*,

New Delhi: Vikas.

Nathans, B., 1990, *Habermas's 'Public Sphere' in the Era of the French Revolution, French Historical Studies,* 16(3), 620-644.

National Perspective Plan for Women 1988-2000, Report of the Core Group Set-up by the Department of Women and Child Development, Ministry of Human Resource Development, 1988, New Delhi: Government of India.

Nelson, Barbara, and Choudhary Najma, 1997, (eds.), *Women and Politics Worldwide*, New Delhi: Oxford University Press.

Oakley, Ann, and Mitchell, Juliet, (ed.), 1986, *What is Feminism,* Oxford, U.K.: Basil Blackwell Ltd.

Omvedt, Gail, 1987, "Feminism and the Women's Movement in India", (mimeo), Bombay: SNDT Women's University.

—, 1988, "Women and Violence", paper presented at the Fourth NCWS, Vishakhapatnam.

Page, Benjamin, and Shapiro, Robert, Y., 1992, *The Rational Public: Fifty Years of Trends in Americans Policy Preferences*, Chicago: University of Chicago Press.

Page, B.I., Shapiro, R.Y., and Dempsey, G.R., 1987, "What Moves Public Opinion?", *American Political Science Review*, 81, 23-43.

Palriwala, R., 1989, "Reaffirming the Anti-Dowry Struggle", *Economic and Political Weekly,* No. 17, 29 April.

Pandey, U.C., 1967, *Yajnavalkya Smriti (Yajna)*, (translated), Varanasi: Chowkhmba Prakashan.

Pappu, Shyamala, 1985, *Women Know Your Rights*, New Delhi: Legal Services Clinic for Women and Children.

Parashar, Archana, 1992, *Women and Family Law Reform in India*, New Delhi: Sage.

Patel, Vibhuti, 1989, "National Conference on Women, Religion and Family Laws in India - A Report", T*he Indian Journal of Social Work*, 50 (I), January, pp. 125-8.

Paul, Madan C., 1986, *Dowry and Position of Women in India,* New Delhi: Inter-India.

Petchesky, Rosalind Pollack, 1984, *Abortion and Women's Choice: The State, Sexuality and Reproductive Freedom*, New York: Longman.

Podell, Janett, 1990, *Abortion*, New York: H.W. Wilson Co.

Pound, Roscoe, 1922, *An Introduction to the Philosophy of Law*, London, New Haven: Yale Univ. Press.

Pound, Roscoe,1923, *Interpretations of Legal History*, New York: Macmillan.

—, 1942, *Social Control Through Law*, New Haven: Yale University Press.

—, 1959, *Jurisprudence*, Vol. I, St.Paul, Minnesota: West Publishing Co.

Prasad, Devi, B. and Vijayalakshmi, B., 1988, "Dowry-related Violence Towards Women: Some Issues", *Indian Journal of Social Work*, Vol. XLIX No. 3, pp. 271-280.

Raizada, K.K., 1989, "Dowry Deaths, Suicide and Bride Burning", *Indian Socio-Legal Journal*, Vol. 15 Nos. 1-2, pp. 87-98.

Rajagopaul, G.R., 1982, "Dowry and the Law", *All India Reporter*, Journal section, pp. 49-51.

Randall, Vicky, 1987, *Women and Politics: An International Perspective*, Chicago: Chicago University Press.

Rao, V.V.P., and Rao, V.N., 1980, "The Dowry System in Indian Marriage: Attitude, Expectations and Practices", *International Journal of Sociology of the Family*, Vol.10, January-June.

Ravindra, R.P., 1987, "Struggle Against Sex Determination Techniques: Unfinished Battle", *EPW*, 21, March.

Rhode, D., 1989, *Justice and Gender*, London: Harvard University Press.

Rifkin, J., 1980, "Toward a Feminist Jurisprudence", Harvard *Women's Law Journal*, 3, 83-95.

Rose, Helen, Ebaugh, Fuchs and Haney, Allen C., 1985, "Abortion Attitudes in the US: Continuities and Discontinuities", Sachdev, P., (ed.), *Perspectives on Abortion*, New Jersey: The Sacrecrow Press.

Rosenberg, Gerald N., 1991, *The Hollow Hope: Can Courts Bring About Social Change*, Chicago: Chicago University Press.

Rudolph, Lloyd and Sussane, 1967. *The Modernity of Tradition: Political Development in India*, Chicago: Chicago University Press.

Sandanshiv, D.N., and Mathew, Jolly, 1995, "Legal Reform in Dowry Laws", Jethmalani, R., (ed.)., *Kali's Yug*, New Delhi: Har-Anand Publications.

Sandhu, M.K., 1988, "A Study of Dowry among Working and Non-Working Women", *The Indian Journal of Social Work*, 49(2), April, pp.155-64.

Sandhu, M.K., 1988, "A Study of Dowry Among Working and Non-Workng Women", *The Indian Journal of Social Work*, Vol. XLIX, No.2, April.

Sangari, Kumkum, and Vaid, Sudesh, (eds.), 1989, *Recasting Women: Essays in Colonial History*, New Delhi: Kali for Women.

Sapiro, Virgina, 1994, *Women in American Society: An Introduction to Women's Studies*, California: Mayfield Pub.

Sarkar, Lotika, 1976, "Jawaharlal Nehru and the Hindu Code Bill",.Nanda, B.R., (ed.), *Indian Women from Pardah to Modernity*, New Delhi: Vikas.

—, 1985, "Women and the Law", Annual Survey of Indian Law, New Delhi: Indian Law Institute, pp. 493-500.

—, 1986, "Women and the Law", Annual Survey of Indian Law, New Delhi: Indian Law Institute, pp. 637-651.

—, 1988, "National Specialised Agencies and Women's Equality", New Delhi: Centre for Women's Development Studies.

Sarkar, Lotika, Sivaramayya, B., 1994, (eds.), *Women and Law: Contemporary Problems*, New Delhi: Vikas.

Sartori, G., 1987, *The Theory of Democracy Revisited*, Chatham, N.J.,: Chatham House Publishers.

Saroja, K., Chandrika, S.M., 1991, "Income and Dowry: Some Revealing Connections", *The Indian Journal of Social Work*, Vol. LII, No.2, Apirl.

Sathe, S.P., 1993, *Towards Gender Justice*, Pune, Research Centre of Women's Studies, SNDT, Women's University.

Scott, Jacqueline, 1989, "Conflicting Beliefs About Abortion: Legal Approval and Moral Doubt", *Social Psychological Quarterly* 52:319-26.

Shiva, Vandana, 1995, "Gender Justice and Global Apartheid", *Mainstream*, Vol. XXXIII, September,23.

Sheel, Ranjana, 1999, *The Political Economy of Dowry, Institutionalization and Expansion in North India*, New Delhi: Manohar.

Shramshakti, Report of the National Commission on Self Employed Women and Women in the Informal Sector, June 1988, New Delhi: Government of India.

Siegel, Reva, 1992, "Reasoning From the Body: A Historical Perspective on Abortion Regulation and Question of Equal Protection", *Stanford Law Review*, 261, January.

Singh, Indu Prakash, 1988, *Women's Oppression, Men Responsible*, New Delhi: Renaissance Pub. House.

Sitaraman, Bhavani, 1994, *The Middleground: The American Public and the Abortion Debate*, New York: Garland Publishing, Inc.

Smart, C., 1989, *Feminism and the Power of Law*, London: Routedge.

—, 1995, *Law, Crime and Sexuality: Essays in Feminism*, London: Sage.

Som, Reba, 1994, "Jawaharlal Nehru and the Hindu Code Bill", *Modern Asian Studies* 28.1.

Spender, Dale, (eds.), 1983, *Feminist Theorists*, London: The Women's Press.

Srinivas, M.N., 1984, *Some Reflections on Dowry*, New Delhi: Oxford University Press.

Stein, Dorothy, 1988, "Burning Widows, Burning Brides, the Perils Daughterhood in India", *Pacific Affairs,* Vol. 61, No.3.

Stimson, James, A., 1991, *Public Opinion in America, Moods, Cycles and Swings*, USA: Westview Press.

Stone, Lind, James, Caroline, 1995, "Dowry Bride Burning, and Female Power in India", Women's Studies International Forum, Vol.5, No.2.

Summers, R.S., 1968, (ed.), *Essays in Legal Philosophy*, Berkeley: University of California Press.

Tambiah, Stanley. J., 1973, *Dowry, Bridewealth and Property*, Cambridge: Cambridge University Press.

—, 1973, "Dowry, Bridewealth and Women's Property Rights", Goody and Tambiah (eds.), Ibid, pp. 59-91.

—, 1989, "Bridewealth and Dowry Revisited", *Current Anthropology*, Vol. 30, No. 4 [August-Octoboer 1989], pp. 413-435.

Tatalovich, Raymond and Daynes, Byron W., 1981, *The Politics of Abortion: A Study of Community Conflict in Public Policy Making*, New York: Praeger.

Teja, Mohinderjit Kaur, 1993, *Dowry: A Study in Attitudes and Practices*, New Delhi: Inter-India Publications.

The Alan Guttmacher Institute, 1989, "The Court Edges away from Roe v. Wade", *Family Planning Perspective* 21: 184-187.

The Alan Guttmacher Institute, 1990, "Looking Ahead to 1990-Opportunities and Obstacles", Washington Memo (January 31).

The Alan Guttmacher Institute, 1992, "Bare Court majority reaffirms Roe, but standard for reviewing state laws is relaxed", Washington Memo (July 2) WM11:1-2.

The Alan Guttmacher Institute, 1992, *State Reproductive Health Monitor*, Washington DC: Alan Guttamacher Institute.

The Report of Joint Parliamentary Committee on Dowry Prohibition Act, 1961, 6th August, 1982, New Delhi: Government of India.

Tocqueville, A. De, 1969, *Democracy in America*, G. Lawrence, (Trans.), Mayer, J.P., (ed.), Garden City: Anchor Books. (Original work published in 1835, 1840).

Towards Equality, 1974, Report of the Committee on the Status of Women in India, New Delhi: Government of India, Department of Social Welfare, Ministry of Education and Social Welfare.

Tribe, L.H., 1990, *Abortion: The Clash of Absolutes*, New York: Norton.

Upreti, H.C., and Upreti, Nandini, 1982, "Parental Authority and Attitude of Women Students Towards Marriage and Dowry", *The Indian Journal of Social Work,* Vol.XLIII, No.3, October.

Vashistha, B.K.,1976, (ed.), *Encyclopaedia of Women in India*, New Delhi: Praveen Encyclopaedia Pub.

Vatsa, R.S., 1977, *The Depressed Classes in India*, New Delhi: Gitanjali Prakashan.

Verghese, Jamila, 1980, *Her Gold and Her Body*, New Delhi: Vikas.

Walby, Sylvia, 1992, *Gender Transformations*, London: Routledge.

Wallace, Ruth, A., (ed.), 1989, *Feminism & Sociological Theory*, New Delhi: Sage.

Weissberg, Robert, 1976, *Public Opinion and Popular Government*, New Jersey, USA: Prentice Hall.

Wetstein, M.E., 1996, *Abortion Rates in the US: The Influence of Opinion and Policy*, Albany: State University of New York Press.

Willigen, J.V., and Channa, V.C., 1991, "Law, Custom and Crimes Against Woman: The Problem of Dowry Death in India", *Human Organization*, Vol. 50, No.4.

Women in India: Statistical Profile, 1988, 174.

Zaller, John, R., 1992, *The Nature and Origins of Mass Opinion*, Cambridge, Massachusetts: Cambridge University Press.

Index